SUCCESS IS WAITING

PRAISE FOR SUCCESS IS WAITING

If you are looking to build a sacred relationship with your student, willing to commit to having a long-term impact on your community, and are serious about turning your school, dojo, or dojang into a special place where the student-teacher relationship flourishes over years, even decades, then this is the best book you'll ever find. Study this incredible resource with highlighter in hand.

Stephen Oliver, MBA
CEO Martial Arts Professional, Mile High Karate, and NAPMA
8th Degree Black Belt

Grand Master Buzz Durkin is truly an original thinker who has been able to help grow and revolutionize the business of martial arts while staying true to the traditional teachings of martial arts and its roots. I know that the time and effort he has put into this book will only help the readers to expand their thinking and continue to grow as martial artists, teachers and entrepreneurs.

Dennis Brown
G.M. Dennis Brown Shaolin Wu-Shu Training Centers
Grand Master of T'ien Shan Pai

Mr. Durkin's book is spot-on. I could not put it down. I found it an easy read of tried and tested gold nuggets of info that can be and should be used by any martial art professional. It all comes from years of experience that can only be gained by being in the trenches of student-teacher/teacher-student experiences. A must-read.

David Deaton
David Deaton Karate Studios
8th Degree Black Belt

Mr. Durkin's book, Success is Waiting, is a very simple yet thought-provoking successful story of one masterful and mindful martial artist. Just take his advice and watch your business grow.

Hanshi Joyce Santamaria
Empire State Karate
9th Degree Shorin Ryu Matsubayashi Karate Do

In this truly priceless treasure of a book, celebrated Karate Master Buzz Durkin shares his time-tested and remarkably relevant philosophy of achieving success in teaching and business, and in attaining a life of endless potential and well-being.

Major David W. Kelley (Ret)
New Hampshire State Police
8th Degree Black Belt, Uechi Ryu Butokukai

Success is Waiting is filled with great insights into the finer details and masterful execution that has allowed him to be an industry-leader in student service and retention. If ever there was a secret to long-term business and life success, it can be found in the pages of this book.

Christopher Rappold
Founder of Personal Best Karate
5 Time World Karate Champion

Buzz Durkin has distilled a lifetime of martial arts experience into these deep, essential lessons. His knowledge, compassion for his students, and his sincere belief in the value of principle-based relationships make this book a true treasure. Read this and you will understand what it means to fully dedicate one's life to helping others succeed.

Brian Glick & Gene Dunn
Brooklyn Brazilian Jiu-Jitsu
Gene Dunn's Shotokan Karate Dojo

Not only should all martial arts school owners read this book, but all small business owners should. Whether you have been in business for years or you have just opened up your doors, this book has a ton of information that can help any business owner. An excellent book.

Henry Guidoboni
Owner of Oriental Gateway
Chairman of the World Martial Arts Federation

I'm thankful to Mr. Durkin for writing this wonderful book and sharing his secrets for having a successful martial arts career and for being a positive role model to thousands both in and outside the dojo. I have spent hundreds of hours on the dojo floor with my training partner Mr. Durkin. He is the real deal! Follow his guidelines and you will be glad you did as you will become a more successful martial artist.

Jimmy Maloney
Father of Uechi-ryu in Canada
9th Degree Black Belt

Master Durkin captures "lightening in a bottle" by putting his thoughts, stories, wisdom, and experiences to paper. Through his practice, he has gained a unique insight that allows him now to share the secrets of success in all areas of a person's life. This is a must-read for anyone who is serious about self-development and the development of their team.

Garland Johnson
Professor of Universal Kenpo Karate
9th Degree Black Belt

Success is Waiting is a brilliant guide to successfully running a martial arts school… and developing and maintaining sound and sustainable relationships in your life, … and includes, often humorous, anecdotes spanning more than 40 years of hands-on experience by Durkin Sensei.

Nestor Folta
7 Time World Champion
8th Degree Black Belt

SUCCESS IS WAITING

The Martial Arts School Owner's
Guide to Teaching, Business, and Life

BUZZ DURKIN

Mushin Publishing
Atkinson, NH

Success is Waiting: The Martial Arts School Owner's
Guide to Teaching, Business, and Life

ISBN-10: 0996575804
ISBN-13: 978-0-9965758-0-5

Library of Congress Control Number: 2015945880

Mushin Publishing
2 Commerce Drive
Atkinson, NH 03811
MushinPublishing@gmail.com

Edited by Jessica Reidy
  www.jessicareidy.com
Designed by William Leith
  william.j.leith@gmail.com
Cover Photography by Pamella Pitman: Stasio's Photograpy

Names of students have been changed to protect their privacy.

For my wife, Judy,
and for my late parents and sisters.

TABLE OF CONTENTS

ACKNOWLEDGMENTS

This book has been a labor of love in the making for many years. I have received generous support from so many people to make this book a reality. I want to extend my personal and sincere thanks to:

George E. Mattson, the father of Uechi-ryu in America and my teacher.

The Educational Funding Company and the Cokinos Family, my long-time business partners and friends from whom I've learned so much about business and people.

Aruna Silva, my EFC account representative for more than twenty years who inspires me daily with his kindness and joy.

Jessica Reidy, a great editor with a wonderful understanding of the English language and the ability to match patience and kindness with focus and determination.

Marcus Traynor, my right hand man for over twenty years, whose tireless work ethic and dedication enable us to accomplish so much for the Uechi-ryu world now, and for future generations to come.

Bill Leith, for his sincere and unwavering dedication to this project and for his keeping me on track with all the computer stuff.

Bridget Lanceleve, my girl Friday who always keeps me organized.

Brandon Stickney, the quiet giant who is rock solid and dependable in any situation.

Deborah Curtin, a brilliant author, writer, and martial artist who encouraged me every step of the way to complete this book.

Alan Kenney, my long-time friend and a financial genius, whose brilliant business plan paved the way for the successful materialization of our school and the eventual writing of this book.

The senior instructors of the Uechi-ryu Butokukai, whose loyalty and dedication are second to none, and every student who has given me the privilege of allowing me to be their teacher.

My brothers and sisters on the EFC Board of Directors, each one a proven leader in the martial arts field.

INTRODUCTION

Dear reader,

This book chronicles my fifty-plus years of practicing Okinawan Uechi-ryu Karate and operating a martial arts school for forty-one of those years. On this journey, I've learned that both success in life and success in business are based upon relationships, and proper martial arts training fosters wonderful lifelong relationships with your students, staff, and peers, as well as with those people outside the martial arts world. By sharing some of my stories and philosophies, I hope that you can apply my experiences to your own life so that you can be more successful with your own relationships, both personal and professional.

Martial arts training helped me immeasurably—when I faced life-threatening situations in Vietnam, my training gave me strength and belief in myself, and when I face challenges in my everyday life, my training leads me to a better understanding of people and human nature. Once I became a teacher, I thought if I could help just one person enjoy even a fraction of the benefits I have from the martial arts, then I would be successful. With this book, I have the same aspiration.

Sincerely,
Buzz Durkin
9th Degree Black Belt

"What lies behind us and what lies before us are tiny matters compared to what lies within us."

—Ralph Waldo Emerson

"Success is not the key to happiness. Happiness is the key to success. If you love what you are doing, you will be successful."

—Albert Schweitzer

Section One
The Epiphany

Chapter 1
In the Beginning

Boston, 1966

I was a junior at Boston College working towards my bachelor's degree in business administration. The Vietnam War was really starting to heat up and the country was in chaos. Young men like me had three options: 1. Get a medical or educational deferment, 2. Go to Canada to avoid military service, or 3. Go in the military for a couple of years and do your duty. I was resigned to take the third course of action and get my service over with, so I joined the Army ROTC while I worked on my degree. I figured if I was going into the military, then I might as well go in as an officer. I grew up in a relatively safe upper-middle class environment, in a quaint little town with tree-lined streets and very friendly neighborhoods. I even attended a private Catholic boys' high school where the only violence I witnessed was the wrath of a priest when our homework wasn't completed or we failed our tests. I knew little about fighting and even less about self-defense. Since I was going into the service, I thought it would be good to know something about physically taking care of myself, especially since I'd chosen to join the infantry.

At Boston College, I had an off-campus apartment with three roommates, Bob Guarente, Jim Callanan, and John Fitzgibbons, none of whom had an interest in martial arts, but even so, one day I was able to convince Jim to check out nearby martial arts schools with me. The first school we went to was on the fourth floor of an aging building, a cavernous, decaying structure on the edge of Chinatown in a district that was neither retail nor commercial, but rather something more like 'ancient industrial.' Of course, in those days most martial arts schools were either on the third or fourth floor because that's where the rents were cheapest. By the time we got to the second floor, we were almost knocked over by a powerful stench like a locker room that hadn't been aired-out for months. By the fourth floor, we were gagging. There were very few people in the school and no one came over to greet us, but that was just as well. The place smelled so bad that it was difficult to notice much else about it and we couldn't wait to leave. *Not a good start!* I thought. *Are all martial arts schools like this?*

The next school we went to was on the fourth floor of another old building. As we climbed the stairs, we heard the ungodly screams of someone being tortured. When we reached the door and bravely investigated, we saw a Japanese man wearing a white uniform, a black belt taut around his waist, and a stern militaristic manner. He took a brief respite from yelling out commands at the students seated against the wall to look at us and scowl before returning his shouts to his charges. Naturally, we stayed and watched as he methodically called out his students one at a time, bowed, and then proceeded to kick the living daylights out of them until the student was writhing on the floor, crying out in agony. This explained the ominous screams we heard from the stairwell. My roommate and I looked at each other and, without turning around, slowly backed our way to the door and set a record for going down four flights of stairs. Once we were clear of that place, we started laughing and could not stop for quite some time. Neither one of us could believe the absurdity. Now the hunt for a school was getting interesting.

The next school we visited was on the third floor. *An improvement*, I thought, as we climbed the stairs. We came upon a door with a sign that read, "Hours of Operation 4:00 PM to 9:00 PM." It was 5:00 and no one was there. We thought that was strange, but we had seen far stranger on our journey so far, so we waited a bit before finally trudging back downstairs. We got something to drink around the corner and after we were refreshed and prepared for whatever awaited us, we went back up to see if anyone was there. And still, no one. Nothing awaited us. Finally, a young man about our age came upstairs with a karate uniform over his shoulder. He looked at us very skeptically, as though being there at all was a very odd thing. Jim said hello and the man begrudgingly acknowledged our presence. I asked if he was the teacher. "Teacher," he said, as though the word were ridiculous in itself. "I'm not the teacher, I'm just a student. The teacher only comes when he feels like it, maybe once or twice a week. I just go in and hit the bag."

Jim said, "That sounds like fun." And there was a silence, and then the sounds of our new friend hitting the bag, industriously and alone. We said our goodbyes amidst the many thuds and grunts, and left, shaking our heads.

By this time, Jim was fed up. "Each place we went was worse than the previous," he said, and he wasn't wrong. But I insisted we try this one last place, Mattson Academy of Karate. The ad in the Yellow Pages made it look somewhat appealing because it was the only karate ad in the entire Boston Yellow pages that didn't have a picture of someone getting kicked in the head. I took that as a good omen. And believe it or not, this school was on the second floor. As we walked up the stairs there were no offensive odors to overpower us and no hideous howls foretelling the pain that would meet us. And when we opened the door, we were not met by a lonely and apathetic bag-hitter, but rather, we were greeted by a pleasant woman who said, "My name is Carol, welcome, I am the office manager. Would you like to look around?" We said yes, with a slight sigh of relief, and followed her. Carol went on to say, "We teach traditional Okinawan karate, a style called Uechi-ryu," as she led us inside, and what we saw was utterly different from all we had seen before. The dojo was bright and airy with many large windows, all of them open, and the students looked neither frightened nor absent, but like they were having a good time training. The locker rooms were even clean— not at all a health hazard.

I looked at Jim and said, "This is the place," and he agreed. And then I looked at Carol, "Where do we sign up?" Carol brought us into her office and we each paid her the $30 tuition for our first month's training and $20 for a gi. We were officially karate students and I couldn't wait to start.

We started the next night, and for me, it was love at first sight; Jim hated it from the beginning. I couldn't get enough; Jim lasted two weeks. For our second class as white belts, we sparred with every other student in class, all of whom were either green or brown belts, and we did this for an hour and half straight. I found it grueling and exciting and strange all at once. I loved the thrilling physicality of the art, the rush of doing something I had never done before, and the strangeness of fending off front-kicks, side-kicks, and spinning back-kicks when I hadn't been taught how to do any of those things. Consequently, not knowing any parrying or blocking techniques ensured that I earned a lot of lumps, bumps and bruises, but nothing was going to stop me from getting good at this. My training made me feel like I was in control of myself at a time when none of us had very much control over anything, and I loved that feeling. And I felt as though my training came naturally to me, like my body was made to do this, and that feeling gave me such confidence. That's how I knew that I made the right decision by starting my karate training in preparation for my military service.

Chapter 2
Education or the Infantry?

Through my junior and senior years at Boston College, I balanced my life between studying business and spending at least four nights a week at the dojo, but honestly, my karate training was the only thing that seemed real. The war made my academic work feel shallow and unimportant in comparison. What I learned on the dojo floor was far more important and far more useful, given the way my life was going to play out in the next couple of years. Reminders of the war were everywhere, on the television; in every newspaper, local and national; and in every magazine from *Newsweek* to *Time*. Believe it or not, despite all the time I spent at the dojo, I earned good grades. Soon, the head of the Marketing Department, Dr. Joseph O'Brien, urged me to get my MBA. I was already in two of his classes and we got to know each other pretty well, and for some reason this brilliant, stern, but fair professor took a liking to me. And while a part of me wanted to get my MBA and continue to work with him, that damn Vietnam thing still hung over my head, just like it did for all my classmates. That other part of me wanted to go into the service and get it over with, come what may. How could I really think of graduate school with a tour of duty as an infantry lieutenant next on my agenda?

About three months before I graduated, Dr. O'Brien called me into his office and said, "OK Durkin, here's the deal. I'll give you a full fellowship for graduate school, all expenses paid, and I'll get you deferment from your military obligation if you'll work for me correcting blue books and helping me with research projects. And I'll pay you a stipend to cover your living expenses. That's my offer, but I have to know in the next couple of days. After that, the deal is off the table. What are you going to do?"

Wow. What a surprise. What a shock. What an opportunity. How could I refuse? The offer was too good. But I still had to think about it. I only would be delaying the inevitability of my military service. I talked it over with my parents, and of course for them it was a no-brainer. My father couldn't believe that I was even considering declining Dr. O'Brien's offer. I talked it over with my roommates, especially John who was a fellow ROTC member and soon-to-be infantry lieutenant, and he thought I was lucky to get the deferment and urged me to take it, telling me, "You should do it," with genuine encouragement. He was happy for me. Even so, my head told me it was the right thing to do, but in my heart I wasn't quite sure. But I accepted and, true to his word, Dr. O'Brien made it all happen: a two-year deferment and a spot in the MBA program. And while I was grateful, I wasn't satisfied. The surety of Vietnam loomed over me—I had only put it off for two years.

As planned, first lieutenant John F. Fitzgibbons did not go to grad school. He did not get a deferment. He went directly to Airborne School and Ranger School, served in the First Air Cavalry Division, and six months later he was killed on a night ambush in Tay Ninh province, South Vietnam. Boy, did I feel guilty sitting safe in my room surrounded by textbooks. Fitzy was dead, and there I was crunching silly statistics, correcting blue books, and taking attendance in the freshman and sophomore classes. Nothing made sense. This was doomsday. John's death made the study of self-defense much more pressing than studying for a degree that I never thought I'd get the chance to use.

Dr. O'Brien noticed this shift in my priorities. He'd tell me, "Durkin, you're spending more time doing that damn karate stuff than you are doing your reports," but still, he was patient with me. He understood that I was grieving, that I felt conflicted and guilty about my deferment. He saw that I struggled to pay attention, that

I was not as thorough with my projects as I was before John died. He knew John as well, and knew that his death weighed on everyone who knew him. It weighed on him as well. He told me that John's death was a waste, and it was. But Dr. O'Brien was a hard task master, and maybe it was best to throw myself into work. Under his direction, time went by quickly, and as it passed, the benefits of karate training manifested more and more in all aspects of my life, far beyond physical fitness. Karate helped me regain my focus so I could complete my thesis, it gave me confidence to defend my thesis, and it kept me calm when I gave presentations to students and business men and women. In this way, karate helped me earn my MBA. And then my deferment was over. I was put on active duty.

In September of 1969, just before shipping out for my first duty station as a new second lieutenant, my sensei, George Mattson, told me to come down to the dojo and to be prepared to test for my shodan, or first degree black belt. His teacher, the world-famous master Ryuko Tomoyose, was visiting from Okinawa and would be sitting on the test board, and it was a great honor for us. The usual black belt testing was conducted in November, but the school changed the testing date to accommodate me and one other student from Rhode Island whose teacher was on the testing panel as well. We didn't spend much time with the famous Mr. Tomoyose, but in those moments that I met him, he was very cordial yet remained serious, and his presence on the panel put a lot more pressure on all of us. We were rigorously tested on the eight core elements of Uechi-ryu. Finally, the test culminated with strenuous, hard-contact sparring, and these were the days before safety gear was popularized in martial arts schools, so we had a painfully authentic experience. My fellow candidate and I were asked to go into another room while the panel discussed our performance. After what seemed like an eternity later, we were asked back in and told that we both had passed. Elated and relieved, we knew that all our hard work and devotion had paid off, and I was proud of myself. Earning my black belt was something real and concrete that I had done to prepare me for the uncertain future. I was as confident and motivated as I could be to take on the challenge of war, waiting just days ahead.

The army has strange ways. Naturally, I was sent to Colorado Springs for cold-weather training to prepare for a year in the heat and jungles of Vietnam. After ten months in Colorado, my orders came through to ship me to Vietnam with a stop-over in Panama for three weeks of intensive jungle training school. I went home for my two-week leave, and said surreal goodbyes to my family and friends, all the while wondering if I'd ever see these folks again. Time rushed forward. I decided to go back to the Mattson Academy for some last-minute training sessions.

It was something I could do to feel more in-control of the uncontrollable. On my last visit to the dojo, my sensei put his arm around me and said, "Don't worry, Buzz. All our black belts have done well over there. You'll be fine." And you know what? I believed him.

Chapter 3
The Epiphany

Phouc Long Province
The People's Republic of Vietnam, 1971
Mobile Advisory Team 18

There were only three of us: Sergeant Turner, our heavy weapons expert; Sergeant McCabe, our team medic; and myself. The other two members of our team, Lieutenant Smith and Sergeant Hedges, were on R&R and emergency leave respectively. Even our battalion of South Vietnamese regional forces was depleted. In total, we were down to about 80 men.

I was now a First Lieutenant United States Army Infantry and team leader of Mobile Advisory Team 18, Military Assistance Command Vietnam (MACV). Our mission was to assist and advise South Vietnamese Regional Force troops in our province. We supplied medivac airlifts and gunship support for their operations to rid the province of Viet Cong and North Vietnamese regular troops. The five of us lived in a small compound recently built by a Special Forces A-Team. They moved out and my team moved in, surrounded by miles and miles of jungle with no easy way in or out but through the air.

We were all exhausted having spent the last three days hacking through the bush. On our first day out, we were ambushed in a Michelin rubber plantation once owned by the French. The plantation stood as a dark reminder— like the roots of the destructive forces of colonization that grew and grew and dropped the seeds for all of this chaos, the chaos that had me crouching behind a rubber tree, calling in artillery coordinates to a U.S. fire base within our Area of Operation while AK-47 rounds zinged past my cover. The chaos that had me saying to myself, "I'll never buy another Michelin tire as long as I live."

Day two was uneventful, marked by a lot of hacking through the jungle.

On day three, we came upon our objective: a bicycle factory. Yes, believe it or not, a Viet Cong bicycle factory, shaded under triple-canopy jungle so thick it blocked out the sun. The Viet Cong had been loading up the bicycles with hundreds of pounds of supplies and equipment and walking them down South on the Ho Chi Minh trail. After minimal resistance and light contact, we took over the factory, which was comprised of caves and tunnels carved into the earth. After we blew-up most of the bicycles and cut out a landing zone, we sat waiting for the Huey Slicks to pick us up and take us back to our compound. As the choppers descended, thumping in to airlift us out, I thought, *What a weird place to be and what a strange thing to be doing, destroying bicycles in the middle of the jungle.* I managed to jump on board the last chopper but I was too exhausted to enjoy the exhilarating ride back among the treetops.

That very same evening, we received our nightly encoded message from Province Headquarters before night had completely fallen. Sergeant Turner and I sat there with our encryption sheet and right from the start we knew it wasn't good. Slowly, we translated the CAC code and stared at each other with grim resolve and no small degree of anxiety. It read, "Intelligence reports tonight 2,000 North Vietnamese regulars to attack your position. No American troop support available. Take appropriate action."

It was a short, hair-raising message, stated so simply. No American support and our team down by two members. Our Vietnamese troops were depleted and those that were left were worn from our recent sojourn into the boonies, destroying all the bicycles we could get our hands on. And now we were about to face 2,000 North Vietnamese regulars, hardened soldiers who had been working their way South.

We informed everyone of our message and began preparations for any eventuality. No one slept that night; everyone was on the perimeter. We checked the wire and put in more claymores. We called the nearest U.S. base and tried to get air support. We made sure our fire arrow was operational and able to turn 360 degrees so the gunships would know where to lay fire. We called in our outposts. We made an escape and evasion route and had a rallying point in the jungle in case we were overrun. What more could we do?

But still there was something missing. After making sure that all was in order, I felt that there was one more thing for me to do, and so I went down into an empty bunker all by myself, where my sensei's words echoed, "Don't worry Buzz, all our black belts have done well over there; you'll be fine." I proceeded to perform my Sanchin kata, the foundation exercise of Uechi-ryu karate. *Sanchin* means *three conflicts*, or *three struggles*, and the student is meant to harmonize mind, body, and spirit through the practice. I did the kata with my entire soul, connecting with something deep within myself: a powerful calmness that I had never before experienced. And despite being saturated with perspiration, when I emerged from the bunker, I sustained that state of peace. Uechi-ryu karate and the Sanchin kata had become a part of me. I knew there was nothing more I could do in this situation, or in any situation, and by letting go of the impulse to control what I could not control, I was ready for anything. We waited.

Chapter 4
Lucky Me

I've always maintained that I was the luckiest infantry lieutenant in Vietnam. The North Vietnamese troops went entirely around our position that night, no contact whatsoever.

The next day, we could see where they had been but for whatever reason they chose to bypass our compound. I thank God and my mother's prayers for getting me home safe and sound, and for helping me survive the many harrowing and life-threatening experiences that Vietnam had in store for me. After I completed my tour of duty, I wanted nothing more than to get on with the rest of my life.

When I got back to the world, I returned to the dojo to continue my study, and soon I began teaching. Karate training had helped me when I really needed it, and I wanted to share its greatness with as many people as possible. I wanted to help. I enjoyed my work, my classes were always full, and my continued training and my teaching served as an anchor, a stabilizing force that allowed me to readjust to civilian life.

As time went on, I decided to open my own school in March of 1974. People have long since asked me, "Did you have to use your karate in Vietnam?" My answer was and still is, "Everyday!" Over the years, I've learned a lot about teaching and running a school, and I hope that by sharing my stories I can help you make your martial arts journey a more meaningful experience for not only yourself but for all the students you may teach.

Section Two

The Essentials

Chapter 5
The Essentials

- Commitment
- Perseverance
- Confidence
- Passion

What I call the four essentials are the qualities required for anyone to be successful in any endeavor. When you practice embodying these four essentials, I firmly believe that any goal is achievable, whatever it may be. Before we discuss each one of these essentials in more detail, I'd like to tell a story that encompasses all four. I call it, "Surprised by Joy."

When I opened my school in 1974, the times were certainly different. All you needed to do to open a school was find a minimum amount of square footage, usually 1,000 square feet, give or take a few, throw up a sign, and you were in business. It bothered me that martial arts schools were the second class citizens of the health and fitness industry at that time. Beautiful health clubs were springing up everywhere and they had all the amenities: air conditioning, showers, easy access, plenty of parking, proper ventilation….Whereas most martial arts schools were either up three or four flights of stairs in a rickety building that did little to promise its stability, or they were down in the basement with a tile or cement floor for you to smash your body on during training. If you were in a higher-end school then maybe they'd throw a rug over the cement to slightly cushion the cold blows to come. And then there were the integral poles in the middle of the floor or the building's oil burner or furnace that you got to fall into during your sparring matches. In short, there was room for improvement.

I wanted my students to study in a facility they could be proud of, and safe in, and I was determined to make it happen. I decided to build my own facility– a free-standing building with all the amenities, including showers, lockers, air conditioning, state of the art flooring, and well-kept grounds. This became my mission and long-term goal. Why not? Of course it would be hard work, but so what? Martial artists are known for their hard work– aren't they? You certainly can't become a black belt without working hard.

At the time, I was renting 1,800 square feet of what was essentially warehouse property. The space had one door and one window and was situated behind a construction company next to a dozen old, parked ten-wheelers. I made up my mind not to compromise; it would be a facility with the best of everything. I knew it would take a lot—a lot of savings, a lot of planning, a lot of patience, and a lot of commitment, perseverance, confidence, and passion. And a lot of convincing the powers that be, mainly bankers, that I could complete this project successfully and sustain it. I was determined to build a martial arts school that would become an enduring model of what every martial arts school in the country could be.

Even though I was saving up, I knew I'd have to borrow a lot of money to finance my project: a free-standing 8,000 square foot building designed from the ground on up for the exclusive purpose of teaching karate. Only a handful of people in the United States built such a school before, and no one had done it in New England. When I proposed my plan, a lot of professionals, realtors, bankers, and even a few lawyers, looked at me like I had two heads. They said, "You'll never do it. You'll never get the financing. You're dreaming." When I was looking for a piece of land, more than one realtor unabashedly laughed at me when I told them what I had in mind.

Nevertheless, I devised a plan of positive expectancy and positive pre-framing: I would act as if my project was already in the works and nothing was going to stop it from being completed. I would talk to people as though I had everything in place and it would just be a matter of time before I'd conduct my first class in my beautiful new school. I had my own unusual little tactic to get the ball rolling at the local bank. Every time I went to make a deposit or conduct other financial business, I made a point of speaking with the bank vice president, who was also the commercial loan officer. But it wasn't so much speaking with him as it was sticking my head into his office and saying, "I'm going to come to see you someday about building my new school." The first time I did this he didn't even know who I was. I don't think he knew who I was for the first year I did this. But, for years, I kept the same routine every time I went to the bank, rain or shine, regardless of the season. Every time I stuck my head into his office, I said the exact same thing: "I'm going to come see you someday about building my new school." Well, over that time period we became pretty good acquaintances– at least he knew who I was and what I wanted to do. I persevered until I made myself a pain in the you-know-what!

After about four years of this, I went into the bank as usual one day, except that day I was very busy and preoccupied, but of course I don't remember why. All I remember is that was the one day that I rushed into the bank, made a deposit, and rushed out again. As the door closed behind me and I started toward my car, I heard this man come running out of the bank and call my name. I turned around and it was the vice president, saying, "Buzz what about your building? When are you going to come and see me so we can make it happen?"

You could have knocked me over with a feather, let alone a punch. Surprised by joy! I had a key ally in my corner, someone who, at the very least admired my commitment, perseverance, confidence, and passion. I was one giant step closer to having my dream become a reality, and a year from that encounter, it did.

Chapter 6
Commitment

Commitment is an action, not just a word. And commitment isn't simply involvement but a dedication, a total dedication. Anyone can be involved. You could think of it this way, a white belt symbolizes involvement and a black belt symbolizes commitment. But I like how tennis champion Martina Navratilova explains it: "The difference between involvement and commitment is like ham and eggs. The chicken is involved; the pig is committed." Commitment is a willingness to make the sacrifices necessary to accomplishing your goals. You might have to work long hours while others are taking time off, forego purchasing something you love to maintain impeccable credit, or give up personal time to join a service organization like Rotary or Exchange to enhance business relationships and become well-known in the community. Full commitment! And I mean a full commitment.

When I was in high school, I took four years of Latin. I really didn't do that well in it and I didn't enjoy it at the time, but I sure am glad I did it because it's helped me more in life than I ever thought it would. Studying Latin helped me broaden my vocabulary, which certainly helps me in my business dealings and seminar presentations, and I also learned stories and legends about what it means to be a warrior, as well as meditations on human nature. One story I remember in particular is that of Julius Caesar crossing the Rubicon River, which is the origin of the famous quote, "The die are cast." Around 59 B.C.E. Caesar had amassed a great personal fortune, popularity, and outstanding military skills. He became so powerful that the Senate in Rome called upon him to resign his command and disband his army. An ancient Roman law forbade any General from crossing the Rubicon River with a standing army and entering Rome; to break this law was treason. But Caesar chose to cross this river to wage Civil War with Rome, and by doing so, he committed to a course of action which he could not reverse. This monumental transgression was an all-or-nothing dedication to irreversible action—it is the epitome of total commitment.

You must have that same mindset as you embark on your endeavor. After crossing your river, burn the boats. No retreat. Successful completion is the only option.

When my wife Judy and I were obtaining financing for our dojo, I cast the die myself. I had to put our house up as collateral, and if I couldn't make our new dojo a success, we would've lost our home. This was the reason we were able to secure financing for our dream and the bankers saw the degree of commitment we were willing to put into this project. Because of this commitment, I also had to increase enrollment by twenty-five percent, just to pay the mortgage and other new expenses. In one sense, it was scary, but in another sense, it wasn't scary at all because I knew I was going to do it. My father used to tell me, "Don't start vast projects with half-vast commitments," and his words rang in my ears when I took these necessary risks to build my business. I was absolutely, positively, unequivocally, vastly committed. No retreat, and no looking back.

Whatever your dream is, whatever you desire, I'm writing to tell you that you can achieve it if you are thoroughly committed. Stephen Dolley Jr. writes, "A [person] who wants to do something will find a way; a [person] who doesn't will find an excuse." Don't find excuses. Instead, see your venture through till the end. Decide. Commit. Succeed.

Chapter 7
Perseverance

Perseverance: like Winston Churchill, I believe that nothing will take its place. Albert Einstein sees it this way: "You never fail until you stop trying." I don't consider myself a great businessman, nor do I consider myself a great martial artist, but one quality I know I have is perseverance, and it's the core of my teaching philosophy. I never, ever give up on my students, no matter how many speed bumps get in the way of our journey. I work with them until they accomplish their goals. Adopting this mindset will serve both you and your students well.

There's a very famous Japanese proverb, "Nana korobi ya oki," which means, *seven times fall; eight times rise.* That's the type of mentality you have to have to be successful. Our goal for over fourteen years was to build our own school from the ground up, and even though very few people believed in me, I persevered, but with purpose, practicality, and self-awareness. There's a difference between charging blindly ahead and using all the tools and good people at your disposal.

A martial arts school is a wonderful place and usually it is a real melting pot. All types of people study with us from doctors to dentists, from sanitation engineers to home-makers, from artists to politicians, and on and on. I was and still am fortunate to have some very talented long-time students enrolled at my school who are experts in their fields. Two of the key people who worked with me on my project were a lawyer and a financial planner, and both are still my students to this day. They told me on numerous occasions that my perseverance was in part what kept them highly motivated about the project. In business, it's important to surround yourself with bright people who recognize and appreciate the essential business and life qualities: commitment, perseverance, confidence, and passion. Best-selling author Regina Brett writes, "No matter how you feel, get up, dress up, and show up." This is what you need to do, even if you are nervous about your undertaking or feeling the breadth and depth of your inexperience in this career, because the pack follows the lead dog. If you present yourself confidently and professionally and you stay motivated and persevere, then so will those working with you, and you will all feel inspired to give nothing but your best.

Chapter 8
Confidence

Don't we martial arts teachers teach our students confidence? Don't people come to us because they want to be more confident? Then it's up to us to be confident, not just on the dojo floor but out in the world as well. We need to live our art form so we can be better teachers and in turn help our students to better themselves too. There are so many martial arts skills, like strong eyes, calm breathing techniques, good posture, and projecting a peaceful and positive presence that will support all that we do in our day-to-day lives. And confidence is attractive. Practice embodying this unwavering belief in yourself wherever you are, whether you're teaching in the dojo or in a banker's office asking for a million dollar loan.

Believe in yourself even if no one else does. There will always be people who will tell you, *you can't do this* and *you can't do that*. Other people may not want you to succeed for a myriad of reasons that may have nothing to do with you or their concern for your well-being. Maybe they weren't able to pursue their dreams, so as far as they're concerned, there's no reason why you should either. Some people may be jealous or envious of your potential or of your audacity to strive for success. Don't listen to these people or be swayed by what they have to say. Carry on with confidence and, oh, what a wonderful feeling it will be when you succeed, knowing that you were right to have faith in your abilities. If you believe in yourself, you'll take chances, and you're more likely to make things happen. I believe that fortune truly does favor the brave.

The following story has been told and retold in the business community, and it's always been an inspiration to me. A business executive was deep in debt and could see no way out. Creditors were closing in on him and suppliers were demanding payment. He sat on a park bench head in hands, wondering if anything could save his company from bankruptcy. Suddenly an old man appeared before him "I can see that something is troubling you," he said.

After listening to the executive's woes, the old man said, "I believe I can help you."

He asked the man his name, wrote a check, and pushed it into his hand saying, "Take this money. Meet me here exactly one year from today. You can pay it back at that time."

Then he turned and disappeared as quickly as he had come, and the business executive saw in his hand a check for $500,000 signed by John D Rockefeller, then one of the richest men in the world.

I can erase my money worries in an instant, he realized, but instead the executive decided to put the uncashed check in a safe. He thought that just knowing it was there might give him the strength to work out a way to save his business.

With renewed optimism he negotiated better deals and extended terms of payment. He closed several big sales and within a few months he was out of debt and making money once again.

Exactly one year later he returned to the park with the uncashed check at the agreed-upon time. The old man appeared, but just as the executive was about to hand back the check and share his success story, a nurse came running up and grabbed the old man.

"I'm so glad I caught him," she cried. "I hope he hasn't been bothering you. He is always escaping from the rest home and telling people he is John D Rockefeller." And she led the old man away by the arm.

The astonished executive just stood there stunned. All year long he had been wheeling and dealing, buying and selling, convinced he had half-a-million dollars behind him.

Suddenly he realized that it wasn't the money, real or imagined, that had turned his life around. It was the renewed, new-found self-confidence that gave him the power to achieve anything he wanted.

—*Author Unknown*

There is a saying, "Fake it till you make it," and that saying has merit. When you start acting with confidence, you will become confident. I summoned confidence because I had no alternative. I was going to open my school whatever it took, despite other people's disbelief in the possibility of my dream becoming a reality, and my confidence changed their attitudes and behavior towards me. You can do the same, you can be bold, and you can accomplish great things. If you're searching for that one person who will change your life, take a look in the mirror.

Chapter 9
Passion

Passion is what burns in your soul; it's the fire that forges your commitment, perseverance and confidence. Passion sheds light on what you want, what makes you happy, and what you're meant to do, and it warms you from within when you are on the right path. Passion keeps you vibrant. Because I'm passionate about my art, I can honestly say that I've never worked a day in over forty years. I don't consider what I do work: it's what I love, and it's who I am.

Many times through the years students have asked me if I ever get tired of doing the same thing over and over. I always say, "No, of course not. No two classes are ever the same. People who come to study with you are never exactly the same day-to-day. It's always new. It's always fresh, exciting, and challenging, and it's always filled with love in one way or another."

It irritates me when I hear a school owner say he's burnt-out. When someone tells me they are burnt-out, I tell them they should just stop teaching and close their school. Burnt-out? What that means is you must have stopped loving that which you are doing—you've lost that passion. If you don't love what you do, then you shouldn't be doing it. The eighteenth-century French philosopher Denis Diderot writes, "There is only one passion, the passion for happiness." And aren't we happiest when we are doing what we love to do?

My passion for my project nourished my commitment, perseverance and confidence to the point that I never doubted that it would become a reality. Just like confidence, passion makes you radiant and, like a moth to flame, attracts the right people to help you achieve what you want. I've never met a great martial artist who wasn't passionate about his or her art. Keep stoking that fire of passion that dwells within you and you will be amazed how the laws of attraction bring the right people to support you. You were born to be successful, just like every human being was born to be successful. Your passion empowers you to do what you were created to do, so go forth and do it. Heck, if I can do it, then you can.

Section Three

Things to Learn and Remember

Chapter 10
Lessons Learned

Emily Dickinson writes, "If you take care of the small things, the big things take care of themselves." This philosophy is a staple in all our classes because I've learned that the small things really do make a big difference. Most of the topics I cover in this book are "small things," and some may even seem deceptively self-evident in their simplicity, but over the years I've seen that all too often that people forget about the small things, both in business and in life, and forget that life is entirely made up of small things. I've learned many lessons about teaching, and more importantly, about human nature, by taking care of these small things.

Chapter 11
Be Happy with What You Have

*"Flow with whatever may happen and let your mind
be free. Stay centered by accepting whatever you are
doing. This is the ultimate."*

—*Zhuangzi*

The Japanese word *mushin*, means *the mind without
mind* or *no-mindedness*. To reach this state, you must
release attachment to anything that has transpired in the
past, as well as any expectations you have of other people
or the future. Live in the present and don't be bound by
preconceived thought or past prejudice. Be happy with
what you have and enjoy what you are doing in the here
and now. It's easy to tell you to live in and enjoy the
present moment and to free yourself from the chatter of
your mind, but much harder to practice and maintain
this state. I think that I can demonstrate how to practice

mushin much more clearly if I share a story about a time when I suffered from a total lack of mushin.

The year was 1967. There was so much excitement at our school in anticipation of the Uechi-ryu headmaster, my teacher's teacher, Kanei Uechi, coming for his first visit to The Unites States, all the way from Okinawa, Japan, just to watch, correct, and inspire us. I was a beginning student at the time, a lowly green belt, but as excited as anyone. When the day finally came and Kanei Uechi walked into our school in Boston, MA, you could hear the proverbial pin drop. Here was the man whose father was the founder of our system, in the flesh. We had heard stories about him since our first day of training and now here he was right before us, and we were in awe.

The headmaster moved with grace and a sizable entourage. Wherever he went, senior teachers surrounded him, anticipating his every move and seeing to it that he wanted for nothing. He wore a perfectly tailored Shureido gi, the finest in the world, beautifully embroidered with association patches. The gold stripes of a master embellished both ends of his jet black belt. Despite his age, his hair was raven black and he wasn't wearing glasses. As a junior student, I had very little interaction with him, but he sure did make an impression. I remember wishing I could travel to the headquarters dojo in Okinawa and see the master in his home environment, surrounded by other masters and his many students. What a picture I drew in my mind of the way it would be.

Fast forward four-and-a-half years later: I am eight months into my tour of duty in Vietnam and I have R&R coming up. The rest and relaxation spots were Bangkok, Thailand; Sydney, Australia; and Manila, The Republic of the Philippines, and none of them interested me. All I wanted was to go to Okinawa and train, even if only for a brief time, with the Uechi-ryu headmaster. After all, I was in the same part of the world and when would I be certain that I'd have this opportunity again? I couldn't be certain of anything.

So I requested my R&R to be in Okinawa: request denied. I wrote again requesting Okinawa, and again, request denied. Not deterred, I put in another request, through the chain of command, with a detailed list of reasons why I wanted to go there. I explained how I had earned my black belt, how my training helped me as a soldier, and why this trip meant so much to me. I must have struck a chord, or perhaps the powers that be at Province headquarters just admired my persistence and my performance in the field. Third time's a charm—request granted!

Two days after the approval, I choppered in from the jungle to Tan Son Nhut Air Base in Saigon, hopped on a C-130, and within hours I landed in Naha, the capital city of Okinawa, and prepared for two weeks intensive karate training with Kanei Uechi.

I checked into a hotel in the town of Futenma, very close to headquarters. The next day, I went to the dojo, excited to meet Mr. Uechi and train with the Master. When I arrived, there was no one there with the exception of an elderly man sitting silently, placidly in a chair. He greeted me with a kind smile, and although he didn't speak English, I mentioned my teacher's name and he seemed to understand where I came from and why I was there. He had thinning grey hair and wore big, thick, black horned rim glasses, rather crooked, and a plain white gi that looked comfortable for him, although a bit small. The gi was absent of patches demarking accolades and was tied with an unadorned black belt turning white from fray. The man rose and crossed the room, and when he returned he had another white gi across his arm and handed it to me. I went behind a curtain into a little closet, which was the changing room, donned my gi, and began to stretch out.

I thought he must be Mr. Uechi's assistant or a long-time student who was holding down the fort for the Master. The man was quiet, calm, and very helpful. He watched me practice my forms and made corrections. And that is all we did, for hours, just the two of us.

I returned to my hotel, exhausted, yet looking forward to meeting Mr. Uechi the next day. However, day two was the same as day one: the old man and I carried on the routine from the previous day, and I worked as hard as I could while he wordlessly corrected my every move. He was an excellent communicator that way, despite our language barrier. He had to be a senior practitioner. But once again, I was the only student, and this disappointed me. Sure, it was an oppressively hot August but I imagined the dojo would be different in the summer, busier, livelier. I imagined that many things would be different. Disappointment lingered.

After class, again exhausted, I soaked in a warm bath in my hotel room, wondering if tomorrow I would get to meet Mr. Uechi. Days three, four, five went by with just the two of us following the same routine. On occasion, a youngster or two would appear in class and the old man would watch and encourage them just like he would do with me, but otherwise, nothing changed.

In truth, I enjoyed my private lessons with this silent old man, but each day my disappointment grew until I was heavy with it. After all, I gave up a restful R&R to meet and train with the headmaster when I could've been lying on the beach somewhere. There I was, exhausting myself with my precious time slipping away, and still I hadn't met Mr. Uechi. My frustration gave way to depression, and I malingered, feeling sorry for myself. I had no one to speak English with and in my isolation, I wallowed, thinking over and over, *Where could he be? Why isn't he here? Is he visiting another country?* Resentful of spending all my time with this one teacher who I neither knew nor could speak with, I lost focus during my training sessions Instead, I shifted my attention to the cold fact that I would not realize my dream of training with the headmaster at his home dojo.

In the second week of my R&R during an afternoon training session, the old man somehow conveyed to me I should come back later that night for an evening class. And of course, I did. Apparently, it was a night scheduled for testing. I arrived early, as always, and already the dojo had more people in it than I'd seen yet. By the time class started, the room was full and there were several other U.S. service people in attendance. Boy, was I happy to see them! After we completed the warm-up exercises, I paired off with one of them, a Marine who had just recently begun his karate training, and we began to stretch. I told him that I had been here for almost two weeks and was heading back to Nam in three days' time, and I admitted that I was a little frustrated and disappointed because I came here to meet Mr. Uechi and it just had not happened.

"Who you been training with, man?" he asked. I pointed to the old man at the front of the dojo. The Marine looked at me incredulously, "Man, that's him— that's Mr. Uechi. You didn't know?"

I had been training with the Master, one-on-one, every single day.

Now, I could blame my ignorance on a dozen things. I could blame my memory of the Master from just four and a half years earlier: black hair and a more youthful face, an exquisite gi, an elaborate belt, and an entire entourage of martial artists. I could blame my expectation of how the Master would be treated in Okinawa, much like I saw him treated on his visit to the United States. I could blame combat stress or my mental and physical exhaustion. None of that is important though. What is important is that this incident taught me to appreciate what I have, to live in the present, and not to let preconceived ideas and expectations prejudice me or negatively color my thoughts, feelings, experiences, and conclusions. This trip was a lesson about the importance of practicing mushin, which is essential not only for my own study, but also for my teaching, and most importantly for my life as a whole.

As the years went by, I developed a wonderful and unique relationship with Grandmaster Uechi. Fourteen years later, he returned to The States for his second and final time, and my dojo was one of two that he personally requested to visit. His visit to our school was such a beautiful and heartwarming experience. He was the personification of altruism—he adjusted folding chairs for two elderly visitors watching class and he encouraged every junior student by either shaking their hand or giving them a gentle and loving tap on the head. While addressing the students at the end of an adult class, he never spoke about himself or his massive achievements. Rather he spoke of the benefits of martial practice and how we all could benefit by making them a part of our lives. After classes, Mr. Uechi and his wife, Mrs. Shige Uechi, visited our home where we enjoyed a wonderful cookout of grilled surf and turf. Mrs. Uechi was so helpful that you would have thought she was the host. She wanted to help Judy prepare and serve everything. And Mr. Uechi was so polite and considerate; he told us he loved the grilled fish and he bonded with Judy by playing with her cats.

Chapter 12
Greetings are Important, but be Careful

Of course it's courteous to greet everybody who comes to your school by name, which is, as I'm sure you know, the sweetest sound to any human being. But greeting people properly consists of a lot more than simply using their names, and over the years I've learned to greet people carefully.

There may be times when you're so busy taking care of your many students and their family members that you can't afford to get into a long, drawn-out conversation with any one individual. It just doesn't make good sense. You're trying to provide the best possible service to everyone in your school, make a personal connection with each student, and cultivate an environment of health and happiness, and you're trying to do this with limited time and resources

I've learned that the best way to do this is to avoid asking open-ended questions. Instead of asking, "How are you today?" and inviting a litany of complaints or stories, greet your students with positive statements: "Gee, it's great to see you," "Thanks for coming to the dojo," "I'm happy you're here," "Have a great time today. You'll learn a lot," or, "Thanks for taking time out of your day to come to the school. We have a great lesson plan for you today." Statements like these enable you to connect with each student personally within a reasonable time-frame for both of you, and they go a long way towards creating a friendly experience and environment for everyone.

Unfortunately, I learned this lesson through this absolutely true story. One afternoon, I sat alone in my office before the day's classes began and a car pulled up. It was one of our first-degree black belts who had stopped training maybe five years prior, and I was happy to see him. As I opened the front door, I quickly recalled a few details about him and his family. Before he even stepped inside the building, I said, "Tim, how are you doing?"

"Not so good, sensei."

Oh! I wanted to change the subject—I cared about his well-being, but I couldn't get into a long discussion about the negative issues plaguing him these last five years. I had to prepare for the start of the day. So I thought I'd lighten the tone and ask about his wife. "How's Lucy doing?"

Tim looked at me with big, forlorn eyes. "Lucy is divorcing me."

Oh dear, I thought. *This is not going well. Think fast, Durkin.* I remembered that his pride and joy was his daughter, Dianne. "How is Dianne doing?"

It was as though I could see his heart deflate as he said, "Lucy has a restraining order against me and I can't see little Dianne."

Now I was really grasping at straws. *Think fast, Buzz, think fast.* The only thing that came to mind was his tiny Chihuahua, Taco. He took that little dog with him everywhere, which was quite a sight considering that Tim was 6'5 and about 230 lbs. Even when he attended class, Taco would wait for him in his car. He loved that dog, and so, in a last-ditch effort to lift his spirits, I asked, "How's Taco?"

He looked at me as sadly as I've ever seen anyone look and said. "Taco died."

After thirty seconds of conversation, before this young man was even five feet inside my building, I made him relive every awful thing that happened to him in the last five years and speak them aloud. Way to go, Durkin!

I learned my lesson.

Of course, there is a time and place for those types of discussions. It's important to be compassionate. But your greeting, however, should be just that, and should encourage health, happiness, and positivity. After all, that's why your students are there to see you—to feel better about themselves.

Chapter 13
Focus on the Positive

Always stay focused on the good things in life. You know that the positives far outweigh the negatives almost any day—consider how many exchanges, how many moments you have during the day that are perfectly benign, even nice, but you probably don't reflect on them in the same way you reflect on those rarer unpleasant moments. Human nature being what it is, however, we tend to dwell on the negatives, perhaps because they upset us, but to some degree, your reaction is a conscious choice you've made.

The real karate master in my household is my wife, Judy. She is an accomplished martial artist in her own right and has been studying Uechi-ryu karate for over forty years. One night I came home from the dojo, very grumpy, and complaining to Judy about an incident I had with this one particular student. "You won't believe what he said to me…You won't believe how the student acted… You won't believe this... You won't believe that....” I went on and on. Finally, Judy looked at me with a stern face and asked, “How many people went to the dojo today?”

“One hundred and fifty-one.”

“And how many wonderful, nice, positive students were in?” she asked.

I knew where she was going with this now. I told her, sheepishly, “One hundred and fifty.”

“Imagine that!” she said. “One hundred and fifty people, all positive, all good, all receptive, and the last hour all you have been talking about is the one negative person.” Then she said, “Snap out of it!” like Cher says to Nicholas Cage in *Moonstruck* when she smacks him across the face. Smart and charming, she was absolutely right.

She really made me consider my own behavior in a new light. Why was I focusing on the one negative when there were one hundred and fifty positives? I always try to keep this conversation with Judy in mind when I start to feel overwhelmed by negativity. A popular, anonymous quote spins it this way, “A bad attitude is like a flat tire. You won't get anywhere until you change it.” Focus on the positive, and heck, it's more fun!

Chapter 14
Don't Listen to the Naysayers

When I went about my journey in southern New Hampshire to find a place to open my school in 1974, I had done my homework. Southern Rockingham County was the fastest-growing area demographically in all of New England. Plus, I could still live at home and drive the forty minutes or so to the dojo. Yes, I was still living at home!

I started visiting realtors and told them what I had in mind and how much space I wanted to rent, approximately 2,000 square feet. At the time, there was a very wealthy and influential businessman in town named Paul Garabedian. His family was one of the first families to settle in the town of Salem, New Hampshire. He owned a massive amount of property and every realtor that I spoke with told me to stay away from him: *He'll gouge you for rent. He won't even take the time to talk to you. He'll laugh at you if he even condescends to meet with you. He'll make you feel terrible. You'd be wasting your time.*

In my search, I eventually found a property that looked like it would serve my purposes beautifully. And, yes, of course it was owned by Paul Garabedian. This gave me pause—should I listen to the naysayers? I thought about what people were telling me and what their motivations might be. First, I got the sense that there were a lot of people in town who were jealous of Mr. Garabedian's success, his triumphs, and his holdings. I also noted that not one person who told me to stay away from him had a fraction of the success that Mr. Garabedian had. And even if he was gruff or unpleasant to deal with, that wasn't enough to put me off. I'm a karate guy! I wasn't afraid to go talk to anyone.

I didn't listen to the naysayers. Instead, I made an appointment through his secretary and went to see him. When I arrived at his office, I explained what I had in mind for my school, the research I had done, the community's need for a resource like this, and my vision. He listened to me with a contemplative expression, and after I finished my pitch he looked me right in the eye and said, "It's yours."

We negotiated rent, which was very fair, and I spent fourteen years at that location, building the school and developing wonderful relationships with friends and students. I became one of Mr. Garabedian's best tenants. I was always so glad that I didn't listen to the envious people in town who said I wouldn't have a chance of renting property from him. Mr. Garabedian became both my business mentor and an excellent friend, and I learned quite a bit from him and his success. Although he had a head-start in life, he didn't rest on his laurels or let resentful people affect him. He worked hard and tried to be fair in his dealings with people, and he always spoke so lovingly about his family and put them first over business. What I admired in him was not just his success, but his good character.

When it came time to move to our new facility, I spoke with Mr. Garabedian just before one of our last classes at the old school and decided to ask him a question that I'd had since our first meeting: "Why did you rent to me? I was just a kid starting out with a karate school, and other established businesses, like the bank, were interested in renting that same spot."

He looked at me so sincerely and said, "I just thought of my own sons, and if they were in the position you were in, I'd want someone to treat them fairly and give them a chance." Far from using his power and privilege to gouge me, he used his position to help a less-established professional with ambition and aspiration. And to think that the naysayers told me, *Don't go talk to Garabedian. No good will come of it.* Quite the contrary, only good came of it.

We all have a choice. We can surround ourselves with negative people or we can surround ourselves with positive people. Surrounding yourself with negative people gets you nowhere. They bring you down, restrict your thinking, and they like to make you feel miserable. Don't pay any mind to them. The positive people, however, become mentors, friends, and confidants who bolster you up, help you find opportunities to grow, and remind you of all the good reasons you have to be happy. So be positive, stay positive, and say nay to the naysayers!

Chapter 15
Everybody's Good at Something

It's easy to think you're great at what you do, particularly when you are the expert. Don't forget your students are putting themselves in *your* world. Meanwhile, they each have worlds of their own on the back-burner while they spend this time learning with you. Years ago, when I was a new and young teacher, I had a student who was… well, let's just say he was not very physically capable. He was in his late forties and terribly uncoordinated. If I said, "Do a right punch," then he would do a left kick. He was very frustrating to teach and I have to admit, shame on me, at times I would lose patience with him and think, *How could anyone not get this? How could anyone be so uncoordinated?*

One evening, I was teaching class and the phone rang. I told the class to keep working while I answered it, since there were no receptionists or program directors in those days, that's for sure. Most of the time, I was huffing and puffing into the receiver out of breath because we were training so hard.

It was the governor's office calling. *The governor's office?* I thought. Yes, and they wanted to know if this student was in class. The person calling told me that he tried calling at home and his wife told him where they could find him. *This is really strange*, I thought, but I called the student over so he could take this call. After a brief conversation, he hung up the phone, came over to me, and apologized for having to leave class but said he was needed up in Concord, the capital city.

After he left, I asked one of his friends what was that all about.

"Mr. Durkin, he's the premier electrician in the state of New Hampshire. He knows everything about everything electric and they had a problem up there that only he could remedy and they needed him right away. He is *the man* for all things electrical in the state of New Hampshire."

That struck me like a bolt of lightning. I can barely unscrew a light bulb without hurting myself and here this man was the most talented electrician in the state. And what had he done? He put himself in my world to learn karate. How dare I get upset with him for not matching my expectations? Then I began to imagine what it would be like if I put myself in his world. If I wasn't electrocuted on the first day then I'd probably be fired or killed on the second.

Everybody's Good at Something

So have patience with your students and let go of your expectations. Everybody is good at something, and if you feel yourself getting frustrated, remind yourself that your students are in your world now and ask yourself how you would fare in theirs.

Chapter 16
Primary Focus

Instruction is the essence of what we do, so focus on teaching your students. Your next event or those events on the horizon, or the prospective student coming in later in the evening, perhaps to enroll, are all secondary. You should teach from a state of mushin—empty your mind of the past and future so you can be completely engaged in the act of teaching in the present moment.

Too many schools have a revolving door policy: ten people in this month, eight people out this month... twenty people in this month, twenty-two people out this month. It becomes a vicious cycle. If you focus all your energy on getting new people in, then you aren't focused enough on the people who are already there. Your students can sense your distraction and in turn they will feel disconnected from the learning process. Focus first on the students who have already committed to you and your school. It is better for them and their studies, better for you as a teacher, and better for your business in the long run.

Now, I know we all need new students. They're the lifeblood of our schools. And the fact of the matter is that we're going to lose students regardless of how great a job we do. Even if you were Bruce Lee reincarnate, you still wouldn't keep everybody. We do need new students, but if getting new students consumes the majority of your energy and attention, then the quality of your service to your current students will suffer and it will be much harder to retain the students you do have. But when your primary focus is on your current students, your school grows and prospers, becomes easier to run, and establishes itself as a true institution of learning in your community. Soon, with this type of focus people will be lining up to be a part of it, and you will earn a reputation as a dedicated teacher.

Chapter 17
People See What They Want to See

The great novelist and memoirist Anaïs Nin writes, "We don't see things as they are, we see them as we are." It's best to just accept this simple yet profound truth. People see things through their own eyes and their own experiences with themselves at the center of their own universe, so take it in stride. It's what it is to be human.

I've been very fortunate in my martial arts journey to have many wonderful teachers who I hold in high esteem, but despite our dedicated practice of the martial way, we are all fallible, and politics inevitably play a role in any organization and can color our perceptions. At one time in the history of Uechi-ryu, there were two political factions. The senior and mentor I studied with at the time (not my original sensei) was alienated from one of these factions in Okinawa, and a group of these Okinawan masters came to visit The United States. At one point during their visit, a world-renowned master performed his kata. I thought it was expertly executed but my mentor at the time said, "I wasn't that impressed with that kata. He looked like he hasn't put on a gi in the last five years." I was shocked—it was one of the few times I heard him say anything negative about anyone, particularly an Okinawan master.

Two-and-a-half years after this event, the political landscape had changed considerably and my mentor was now aligned with the Okinawan group from which he was previously alienated. The very same master we'd seen perform the kata visited once more and again performed his kata. After the demonstration, my mentor said "Wow, what a great kata! I've never seen anything like it. Look at the way he moved—catlike and yet so powerful." To my eyes, however, this elderly Okinawan's kata hadn't changed that much at all over these few years.

What had changed was my mentor's perception. He saw what he wanted to see. When he was alienated from this particular Okinawan, his kata wasn't impressive, but after forming an alliance, the Okinawan's kata was very impressive. I don't mean to disparage any of my mentors; rather, this incident made salient the simple truth that we all see from our own eyes. Though we strive to overcome this limitation and be impartial, often we may not even realize our own prejudices because they can alter our perception of reality. So don't take other people's perceptions personally, or, in the popular vernacular of the day, *it is what it is and people see things as they are.*

Chapter 18
It's Not What You Say That Matters, it's What They Hear

And there's very little that you can do about it.

Years ago, I had a student preparing to test for his black belt. He was just a bit overweight. I took him into my office and as gently as possible, I talked to him about what we all know is a very sensitive subject. I told him if he could lose five to eight pounds, he would be in fighting shape and really excel and look his best at his test. He agreed.

But as the months went on, he began to come to class less and less. He was getting out of the habit of regular practice. One night, I asked his girlfriend, "Where is Michael"

"He doesn't want to come to class anymore because you told him he was fat!" she said. "He's self-conscious!"

What a shocker that was to me. I never called him fat—I told him that he looked good and if he lost five to eight pounds he would excel at his test, but all he heard was, "Durkin said I was fat," probably because he was already sensitive about his weight, so any perceived criticism would sound harsh to his ears no matter how well-meaning my intentions were. We all have sensitivities, so when you discuss sensitive subject-matter with your students, they're most likely to hear exactly what they don't want to hear. And remember, as the legendary basketball coach Red Auerbach was fond of saying, "It's not what you say that matters, it's what they hear!" So I suggest being very, very careful when dealing with sensitive subjects, like weight, because it is easy to hurt your students even when you're trying to help.

Chapter 19
Sometimes You Just Can't Win, but Keep Trying

I once had a wonderful married couple at the dojo, both black belts, and both excellent students. One night, the husband asked if he could talk to me after class. (Don't we all love it when someone says, *Can I see you after class?*) He came into my office and explained that his wife was going through a lot of emotional trouble with her parents and he said that she wanted to come in and talk to me about stopping her training for a while. She just needed more time for herself. He asked me not to try to persuade her otherwise. "Be exceptionally tender with her," he said. "She's very fragile." I listened to him and respected his request.

Well, the next night his wife came in to talk with me. She sat down in my office and said, "Mr. Durkin, I'd like to take some time off from training. I have a lot going on and I need a little time for myself." Without batting an eye, I told her, "Go right ahead. I totally understand. We will miss you but the dojo will be here when you come back. I look forward to your return."

I thought I handled it beautifully.

Three days later, her husband came in to the dojo and asked, "What did you say to her?"

I reassured him, "I said very little and did exactly as you had requested."

"Well she couldn't believe that you didn't even try and talk her out of stopping. After being here six years, you just said, 'Okay, go ahead. Take time off.' You didn't even try to get her to stay in class. She thought she couldn't mean very much to you."

I looked at him and did not know what to say. I tried my best in that situation but it was darned if I do, and darned if I don't. That's okay. That's all part of being a teacher, isn't it? When things like this happen to you, dust yourself off, get back in the saddle again, and continue trying your best.

As teachers, we are dealing with the most fragile of things—the human condition. We are entrusted with the human spirit, a resilient yet very delicate force. Everyone has a heart, a soul, feelings, and emotions. Take good care of those in your care and tutelage. Do your best with each and every person who crosses your path, and really, that is all you can do. Over time, you will be rewarded in spades for doing so, even when the cards are stacked against you.

Chapter 20
Sometimes You Just Have to Say Goodbye

Sometimes saying goodbye is a gift, both to yourself and the other person. People are funny and things are not always going to work out. No matter how hard you try, you just cannot please everyone. Understanding this is very important. People bring their own baggage with them wherever they go. If a relationship with a student goes poorly, it may have nothing to do with you. What is important is that, at the end of the day, you can look yourself in the mirror and say, *Yes, I acted with integrity and I've done my best.*

I remember one introductory class I taught: I thought the class went beautifully, and we had a prospective student that day, a young girl whose mother watched with little expression. When I sat down and spoke with the mother during the enrollment conference, she was very confrontational, even bordering on belligerent.

Every time I went to make a point about our program, she had something negative to say. She actually began telling me how I should be running things. I listened politely and then I explained how our school worked, and with a roll of her eyes, she told me she would think about it.

Before going home that evening, I went over what had transpired and it seemed like she may not be happy enrolling her daughter at my school. Of course you want new students, but to be successful, you want them on your terms. I wrote a note to the mother stating that our job was to make people feel good about themselves and not to make people upset, and that our school didn't seem like a good fit for her. Along with my note, I included the check she had given me for our introductory program. I wished her all the best and thanked her for visiting. I felt good about myself after that because I sincerely thought it was the right thing to do. For a student to come into your school, it has to feel right for everyone, and if it doesn't, then there could be a lot of agony down the road for you and for the student. This particular story, however, had a happy ending.

Two days later, I received a call from the very same mother asking if she could make an appointment to see me. I told her, "Of course." When she met with me, she said that she was shocked that I would not accept her daughter and that I had refunded her check.

Then to my surprise, she did a total one-eighty and changed her demeanor, explaining that the day we met she was dealing with a lot of negative issues in her life and that was reflected in her attitude towards me and our school. She acknowledged her belligerence, apologized, and asked if I would give her another chance and accept her daughter for enrollment. I said that I would, and I did. And her daughter stayed with us as a student for eight years. The mother also later became a student studying with us for ten years!

When you really think about it, we are only martial arts instructors. We don't all have PhD's, we are not all doctors, nor are we all certified therapists. Our job is to teach people how to be healthy in the martial way. Sometimes people will come into your school and they might be in need of more help than your dojo can provide, regardless of how much you try. In the 60's and 70's, I saw that a lot of troubled people were attracted to the martial arts because they believed that martial arts training would be the solution to every problem they had. Sometimes I still see this. Mostly though, the people who come to us are emotionally and mentally stable and want to study the martial arts for the right reasons.

Sometimes, it may simply be that the timing isn't right for a particular student. There have been many occasions when, no matter how I tried to communicate with a student, we just didn't connect. Often, students of this ilk came back two, three, even ten years later when the timing was right for them and they became good students.

Sometimes it's hard to say goodbye. But if things aren't going well, please remember, it's better to have a crisis than a lingering bad situation. When I've had to let someone go, either a student or a staff member, typically my first reaction has been, *Why the heck didn't I do that sooner?* You'll feel the same way too. So don't be afraid to say goodbye. The key to any relationship is to act from a place of strength. I'm not talking about physical strength, I'm talking about moral courage, integrity, and the strength to do what you know in your heart is right. You're a martial artist. Be brave.

Chapter 21
More is Caught than Taught

"A man who has attained mastery of an art reveals it in his every action."

—*Samurai Maxim*

I maintain that you teach more off the floor than you do on the floor. People observe you when you're talking to someone outside of class, when you're on the phone, when you're at the gas station, the car wash, and the supermarket.

If you talking about patience, for example, and give a wonderful homily on how patience is important for your training and in your life, and then after class a little yellow belt asks you to tie his belt and you blow him off because you're busy with something else, then your homily on patience was a waste of time.

Teaching the curriculum is one thing but modeling the proper behavior of a spirited martial artist is another.

Don't be one way on the mat and another way off the mat. To be really masterful, there is no difference between you and your art. You become your art, and your art becomes you. The way you act in the world should be how you act at your school. This is how we truly teach.

On one of my trips to Okinawa in the late-1970s, I was practicing at the Headmaster's dojo. It was fascinating to watch him observe the students so closely and make corrections with such a personal connection between himself and each of his students. I couldn't help but notice how gentle, considerate, and reassuring he was with each and every student. He seemed so natural in all he did. When he performed his kata for the class, it was something beautiful to behold, and his students, in turn, watched him silently, respectfully, and with their full attention.

One morning, after a rigorous training session the previous night, my training partner, Michael Chaille, and I decided to go to the center of town to get some breakfast. Just by luck, two blocks ahead of us was Master Uechi walking with his wife. They obviously were going grocery shopping. And like the mature martial artists we were, we said, "Let's follow him."

We noticed how he greeted everyone with a genuine smile, which they returned. He had a buoyant gate and moved with grace. After a couple of blocks of following the headmaster and his wife, we finally said *enough of this silliness*, raced up, said good morning, and accompanied them both to the center of town. They were genuinely happy to see us and the four of us proceeded to go on a little shopping spree. This small outing felt special and welcoming because of the artful and compassionate way that he and his wife conducted themselves, and we had a great time.

When I returned home to my dojo in New Hampshire, The students asked me, "How did he move? What was he like?"

After thinking about it, I said, "If you saw the man walk down the street, then you saw him do his kata," because I realized that there was no difference between the two. If you saw him do his kata, then you saw him walk down the street. He *was* his karate after training so diligently for so many years. There was no distinction. He was his art; his art was him.

And isn't that the best way to be? Without façade, just be who you are, on and off the mat. If you're sincerely striving to be your best, then you're sincerely being who you were meant to be. Wherever you are and however you behave, your students will 'catch' your behavior and learn from how you conduct yourself. They will strive for mastery if they see it in you. Children in particular are great imitators, so give them something great to imitate, not just at your school, but everywhere.

Chapter 22
Affable and Unflappable

These two qualities will serve you well whether you are teaching your students or interacting with people in your daily life outside of school. Always be affable and unflappable. Yes, that's right, it rhymes and everything: affable and unflappable.

If you're affable then you're friendly, kind, and you're pleasant to be around. People enjoy your company because you have a great spirit. If you're unflappable, then you don't let little things bother you. And if you read Richard Carlson's book *Don't Sweat the Small Stuff…and it's all small stuff,* then you will learn just that—life is all small stuff. Be calm, cool, collected and your students will be amazed at how nothing seems to rattle you.

All the great masters seem to share these two wonderful qualities. If you can be affable and unflappable in all your dealings inside and outside of your school, then people will be attracted to you and want to be around you, and you'll earn a reputation for being kind and level-headed. The more affable and unflappable you are, the more respected you will be.

After all, there is a simple reason why people continue to study with you: they like you. If they didn't like you, then they wouldn't be there. The more affable and unflappable you are, I guarantee you, the more influence you will have with your students. Generally when people like you, you tend to like them back. This mutual likeability lends itself to a tremendous dojo atmosphere and enhances the entire learning experience.

Chapter 23
When Things Go Wrong

Remember this adage: Don't just go through hard times, grow through hard times. If you're operating a school, or any business for that matter, it's not a question of *if* things go wrong. It's a question of *when* things go wrong. Things-going-wrong is part of the whole business process. If you're not having challenges then you're probably not in business.

We are all going to face challenges, but I've learned that these challenges make us better teachers and better human beings. It's easy to give advice when things are going swimmingly. It's easy to give advice when you aren't in, or haven't experienced, crisis. But I can guarantee that if you can hold your head high and function with integrity when you go through hard times, then you will come out the other side much better equipped to help your students with their own challenges. Granted, as teachers, some of our challenges may be unique from our students' challenges, but navigating your own troubled waters with grace will give you valuable insights that you can share with your charges.

And while you may navigate with grace, nevertheless, troubles can take their emotional toll. For instance, how do you deal with the longtime student, to whom you've given your heart and soul, who decides to leave you and open up another school right down the street? How do you deal with the student who joins another school and actively recruits your students to join this new school? How do you deal with the student for whom you bent over backwards to help and encourage, but leaves you without saying a word and speaks poorly of your school after leaving?

As the old saying goes, you may not be able to control what will happen, but you can certainly choose to control how you react to it, and I firmly believe that life is 10% what happens to you and 90% how you choose to react. The best advice I can give you regarding challenges is to always take the high road and don't lower yourself to the level of the person who has wronged you. Don't waste energy agonizing, plotting revenge, or hanging on. Don't give it any space in your head. Let it go. Instead, focus on the present and how you can make yourself and your school even better. By taking this approach, you absolutely will feel better about yourself and I guarantee you will be happier because you are directing your energy into something positive that you can control. You can control your attitude and your actions. Your ship will right itself in the end. It may help to remember too that the people in your life may be fighting a battle that you know nothing about, and that is something that you can neither fix nor control, but your behavior toward them still matters. So go about your business with character and integrity, never speaking ill of anyone, treating everyone with the same care and respect. Your character is your most valuable asset, and as Norman Schwarzkopf once said, "Leadership is a potent combination of strategy and character, but if you must be without one, be without the strategy."

Challenges test and build your character and often require that you make changes, though change can be difficult, even when necessary. My suggestion is to push past the pain of change. Besides, if something doesn't change us, then it doesn't challenge us, and we don't grow. I believe that if you accept the challenge of change, then you will move forward and be better for doing so, and it's for that reason that I've always loved the following poem, "Don't Quit," by Edgar A. Guest:

When things go wrong as they sometimes will,
When the road you're trudging seems all uphill,
When the funds are low and the debts are high,

Things to Learn and Remember

And you want to smile but you have to sigh,
When care is pressing you down a bit--
Rest if you must, but don't you quit.

Life is queer with its twists and turns,

As everyone of us sometimes learns,
And many a fellow turns about
When he might have won had he stuck it out.
Don't give up though the pace seems slow-
You may succeed with another blow.

Often the goal is nearer than
It seems to a faint and faltering man;
Often the struggler has given up
When he might have captured the victor's cup;
And he learned too late when the night came down,
How close he was to the golden crown.

Success is failure turned inside out-

The silver tints in the clouds of doubt,
And you never can tell how close you are,
It might be near when it seems afar;
So stick to the fight when you're hardest hit-
It's when things seem worst that you must not quit.

Commitment, perseverance, confidence, and passion
will enable you to stay the course when things go wrong.
By acting with integrity and character and by taking the
high road, you will come out better than before.

Chapter 24
Don't Put Labels on Money

Never qualify money by saying it's "only this" or it's "only that." A hundred dollars to one person may be pocket change while to another person it could be all the money he or she has in the world. But a hundred dollars is a hundred dollars; it's not *only* a hundred dollars.

When I first opened my school, it was a financial struggle and I had very little discretionary income. As a new business in town, I was contacted by a very well-established business leader who was recruiting people for the Chamber of Commerce. He wanted me to join, told me of its benefits, and added, "And besides it is *only* a hundred dollars." Well, a hundred dollars to him at the time was not much money. He actually drove around town in a Rolls Royce. But to me, it was a lot of money and I didn't have a hundred dollars to spend on joining the Chamber. I told him I would think about it.

That incident struck a chord with me because I felt a little inadequate. I didn't have the money and the words "*only* one hundred dollars" repeated over and over in my mind. I made a mental note of never qualifying a sum of money like that to anyone. I wanted to be sure that no one feels the way I did because of how I present the price of something. Money is what it is—nothing more and nothing less.

Chapter 25
It is Your Conviction That Makes it Happen

All great martial artists believe 100% in what they do. They have an unwavering belief in what they practice and what they teach. Your belief in what you do is what attracts students and motivates them to improve.

Students see in you certain qualities that they would like to emulate. If you help them to realize that you developed these qualities through your martial arts training, then they will want to do the same. *Selling* may be a crass term to some, but as Zig Ziglar writes, "Selling is a transference of feeling," and this is especially true in the martial arts. If you believe deeply in what you do and have firm conviction in its importance, then your students will believe deeply in it too. It's that simple. People who visit my school can't believe we have a traditional curriculum of only eight kata and yet have remarkably outstanding retention. The reason is that transference of feeling. Hopefully, my students see that I've cultivated any positive qualities they might see in me through my Uechi-ryu practice, and realize that they can use the very same curriculum to encourage and embody these qualities as well. In this way, we all practice strength, patience, confidence, coordination, technical skills and on and on as a community and improve together.

So many teachers fall for the martial art du jour. Back in the 70s when the TV show *Kung Fu* aired, featuring Kwai Chang Caine, some schools took down their signs advertising whichever style of martial arts that they were teaching and replaced them with signs that read "Kung Fu" even though a lot of these teachers never even studied Kung Fu. And years later when professional kickboxing was en vogue, the Kung Fu signs came down and the PKA signs went up. And while so many dojos in the United States play on the trends, I maintain that it's really not what you teach that's the key to your success. If you're teaching something that's credible, that has validity and that is real, then it's your belief in what you do that will keep students coming to you, staying with you, and benefiting from what you have to offer. But if you're flipping around from pillar to post every time another martial arts system becomes popular, then your students will have little faith in what you have taught them and this behavior certainly does not bode well for retention. And we want good retention because we know the longer we keep students with us, the more they benefit which in turn benefits your community and society.

Great teachers know how to disguise repetition to keep classes interesting and fun, and a firm conviction of quality over quantity is imperative for great instruction. It was Mohammed Ali who said, "It's the repetition of affirmations that leads to belief. And once that belief in what you do becomes a deep conviction, things begin to happen." Believe wholeheartedly in yourself and in what you do and your confidence will shine through. Don't worry about what the guy down the street is doing or what's 'in' at the moment.

Section 4

Teaching Tips

Chapter 26
Key Teaching Tips

Everything revolves around good instruction, especially the ability to connect with and understand your students, as well as the skills to create successful events, programs, activities, and social gatherings. Outstanding instruction is the backbone of a great martial arts school, and without it, all of your efforts and promotions will be for naught. Make it happen on the floor. Focus on becoming a better teacher and finding better ways to communicate with your students. Your school will thrive and grow to be an exciting place to learn, and you will grow too.

Chapter 27
Instructor's Code of Ethics

The Oxford English Dictionary defines *ethics* as, "the moral principles or system of a particular leader or school of thought; the moral principles by which any particular person is guided." The same dictionary defines *morals* as, "habits of life with regard to right or wrong conduct."

As martial arts teachers, how do we define what we do? Are we under an obligation to teach ethics or a moral code of conduct? Or is our job just to teach our students how to defend themselves?

I'm willing to bet that you agree with me that a code of conduct is essential to what we do. Can you imagine what kind of society we would live in if we only taught our students to fight and gave little regard to conflict resolution or the proper use of self-defense? Imagine the chaos we'd live in if physical strength determined right from wrong.

Ours is a noble profession. We give of ourselves to teach others how to defend their lives and the lives of their loved ones. As such, we should teach, expect, and model ethical conduct as an integral part of the martial arts. Demand that your students conduct themselves ethically just as you demand the meticulous execution of a sidekick or an arm-bar, because with martial arts ability comes responsibility, and the greater our ability, the greater our responsibility. The most progressive modern-day martial artists and school owners are using a curriculum that makes it easy for us to teach proper behavior and personal responsibility, particularly through keystone texts like the "The Student Creed" and "The 8 Virtues of Black Belt."

"The Student Creed," by the late Chairman of the Educational Funding Company Nicholas Cokinos:

> I intend to develop myself in a positive manner
> and avoid anything that would reduce my mental
> growth or physical health.

> I intend to develop self-discipline in order to
> bring out the best in myself and others.

> I intend to use what I learn in class constructively
> and defensively to help myself and my fellow man
> and never to be abusive or offensive.

Can you imagine how peaceful our lives would be and how much healthier we would feel if everyone practiced the tenets of "The Student Creed" on a daily basis? We teach our students that mastering technique requires self-discipline, and we also teach the difference between disciplining someone and encouraging a student to develop self-discipline. On the floor, we set an example of how to act by being neither abusive nor offensive. All students, junior and senior, should work together in mutual respect so that respect becomes part of the student as a person, both inside and outside of the school.

"The 8 Virtues of Black Belt"
Modesty
Courtesy
Integrity
Compassion
Gratitude
Self-control
Perseverance
Indomitable spirit

On their own, the virtues can be a little abstract for the students, so I teach my students how to integrate these virtues into their lives inside and outside the school.

Modesty in the dojo: Be humble about how far you've come with your training and realize that there is always more to learn.

Modesty in life: Don't brag about your accomplishments, physical, social, or academic.

Courtesy in the dojo: Treat all students and dojo family members with great respect and politeness.

Courtesy in life: Treat people the way you'd like to be treated, making good manners your first reaction to any situation.

Integrity in the dojo: Be honest in your efforts and your personal work ethic. Be true to yourself and do your best from the moment you 'bow in.'

Integrity in life: Be honest with everyone, including yourself, and always do your best to keep your word to your family, friends, and peers.

Compassion in the dojo: Assist junior ranking students and less-accomplished students and appreciate their efforts.

Compassion in life: Be sensitive to other people's feelings and try to understand their perspectives.

Gratitude in the dojo: Be thankful to your teachers and fellow students for helping you improve.

Gratitude in life: Thank your family members and the people in your life who help you and always show your appreciation.

Self-control in the dojo: Develop self-discipline in the spirit of the Student Creed and strive to be neither too high nor too low.

Self-Control in life: Remain even-tempered especially in times of great stress. Work to maintain physical and emotional balance, for instance, by eating healthily, exercising regularly, practicing self-care, and creating a support system of friends and or family.

Perseverance in the dojo: Even though training is difficult, work hard and rise to meet challenges.

Perseverance in life: Don't quit just because something is difficult. Instead, see things through and consider how challenges may help you grow.

Indomitable spirit in the dojo: "Nana korobi ya oki," or, *seven times fall; eight times rise*. No matter the odds, keep striving to succeed.

Indomitable spirit in life: Have a "Yes, I can!" attitude in every situation.

There's a poem by an unknown author that appears in the book *Wooden* by coach John Wooden that I suggest you read to yourself at the start of each teaching day to remind you of the best way to make a difference, one student at a time, by teaching, expecting, and modeling the martial way.

> "No written word—nor spoken plea,
> Can teach our youth what they should be,
> Nor all the books on all the shelves,
> It's what the teachers are themselves."
>
> —*Author Unknown*

Chapter 28
Five Questions

Here are five questions that you should constantly be asking yourself:

1. Am I giving 100% of my best effort to each and every student each and every day?

2. Am I diligently teaching and developing the martial way through study of the tenets of our Student Creed and The Eight Virtues of Black Belt?

3. Is there a sacred space shared between my students and me?

4. Is there a sacred space shared between my students and the people who teach for me and among the student body as a whole?

5. Do I make 2,4,6 calls, attendance calls, send birthday cards, and follow up with my students in other ways because it is a good policy or because I have a genuine concern and care for each and every student?

Sacred space is a term often used in Okinawan karate referring to the unique personal relationship between a teacher and his or her student, and goes hand and hand with the martial axiom: "Between the teacher and the student, there is only the teacher and the student." Work to cultivate mutual respect and a true connection between you and your students.

And "2,4,6 calls" are the phone calls you make to newly enrolled students at the two week, four week, and six week mark to ensure that the student is happy with his or her training, and to answer any questions the student may have.

Keep these five questions in mind and the bond between you and your students will be strong and enduring.

Chapter 29
Five Things Every White Belt Class Should Include

Every beginner's class should more often than not contain the following components:

1. Physical exercise
2. Something practical
3. Something abstract
4. A sense of accomplishment
5. A sense of completion

What does this mean?

Physical exercise: Often times we get so hung up on teaching technique that we forget that white belt students need physical exercise. It should be a big part of what we do and it is a big part of the students' expectations, and in many cases it is why they are with us. Stretching as well as strengthening exercises like planks, push-ups, and abdominal crunches are certainly beneficial and help your students develop strength, stamina, and control.

Something practical: New karate students for example need to feel like they are learning 'real karate,' which for most new students means something practical like punches, blocks, kicks, and other a self-defense techniques that they may have been exposed to through books, movies, or T.V.

Something abstract: The martial arts are steeped in 'mystical' concepts and glorious legends of the founders and their accomplishments. Stories about Gichin Funakoshi, Morihei Ueshiba, Kanei Uechi, Helio Gracie, and others can fascinate and inspire new students. They will be intrigued by these stories and philosophies and if you can share them with passion and conviction then they'll relish the opportunity to explore new territory and a culture they may not otherwise have been familiar with.

A sense of accomplishment: If you acknowledge your students' progress then they know when they're 'getting it.' Praise is just as important as correction. The repetition will never feel in vain if your students are taught to recognize their own improvement.

A sense of completion: White belts can be easily overwhelmed and need a sense of order in their training. Make sure that your lessons come full circle by the end of the class and tie everything they've learned together. Your students need to have a sense of what they accomplished over the last sixty minutes.

Chapter 30
The Sensei's Job

The sensei's job is really quite easy and can be summed up in five words: *provide the proper dojo atmosphere.*

Think about it, that's really all that has to happen. Martial arts training is a journey of self-discovery. The teacher isn't meant to spoon-feed the curriculum. As a matter of fact, a famous martial arts maxim maintains that "[t]he more I teach you, the less you learn."

However, providing the proper dojo atmosphere encompasses quite a bit and ideally you want to create an environment in which the students teach themselves and each other. Ask yourself, are the students working hard? Are they working cooperatively? Are they participating with the spirit of the martial arts? Are seniors helping junior students? Are junior students being respectful? Is everyone trying their best? Are you modeling and encouraging these behaviors? Your answers to these questions will show you where your atmosphere needs attention and what is already working well. Cultivating a cooperative community will help your students realize that they will reach their fullest potential if their classmates improve too. The stronger the individual grows, the stronger the class grows as a whole, and vice versa. You want your students to learn organically by observing how you interact with each and every one of them, by collaborating with their fellow students, and most importantly, by discovering more about themselves.

Chapter 31
Three Key Elements

It's the teacher's function to guide students in fostering commitment, diligence, and patience through the martial way. These three key elements are essential to the study and practice of the martial arts.

Commitment: I realize we've discussed the importance of commitment in business earlier, but the type of commitment I'm speaking about here is martial commitment. As a teacher, if you don't ask for a commitment from your students, how can they be successful? They need to commit to dedicate several hours to practice at the school and at home every week. I know quite a few teachers who are afraid of asking for this commitment and make it much too easy for the student to quit training as soon as an obstacle or challenge gets in the way. Martial training is serious business. We're talking about developing the skills to defend one's life.

Yes, as excellent teachers we can make it exciting and even entertaining but it can't be all fun and games. It is imperative to commit to working consistently hard.

Diligence: When your students practice diligence, they rise to a higher level of awareness and physical ability because they are carefully and persistently honing their skills. Diligence implies a sense of self-awareness, and so the skills they learn become part of who they are. This kind of alertness enables them to prevent or diffuse conflict before it becomes a situation, or when conflict is unavoidable, they have the physical ability and proper mindset to engage responsibly and protect themselves and/or their loved ones. —Simply put, when a student practices with diligence he or she is aware enough to employ their skills effectively and intelligently.

Patience: Martial arts training takes time, requires hard work, perseverance, and the many other qualities we've discussed, and patience is the virtue that makes this all possible. Patience creates a state of mind necessary to travel the long road of practice and study. Teach your students that they need to practice patience in order to expertly learn a technique or a skill on the mat, just as they need to practice patience in order to expertly handle the troubles that life may throw their way, for instance, when someone cuts them off in traffic or is rude to them at school or work. Patience will guide them through life's difficulties and challenges, and as Napoleon Hill once said, "Patience, persistence and perspiration make an unbeatable combination for success." Remind your students that patience isn't just about waiting, it's about how you wait—your attitude, your actions, and your work ethic.

Help your students embody these three key elements by embodying them yourself; by guiding them when they are off-track; and by praising them when they are acting with commitment, diligence, and patience. The more you help them develop good character, the more meaningful impact you will have on their lives.

Chapter 32
Bread and Butter

My late mentor, Nicholas Cokinos, always told us to practice and teach our "bread and butter," and our bread and butter is what we are best at. In other words, play to your strengths. No matter how many distractions or fads come along, don't be sidetracked by something that isn't your forte.

I heard this story about a man who was walking through the airport and while he was waiting for his plane he saw this machine that said "Fortunes told: 25 cents." He had a little time so he put a quarter in the machine, and the readout said, "Your name is John Smith and you're on the 220 flight to Boston." He thought that was amazing! He couldn't believe it. How did it know?

Just then a friend walked by. "Come here!" he said. "Check this out!" He took another quarter out of his pocket, dropped it in the machine, and there it was again:

"Your name is John Smith and you're on the 220 flight to Boston." Well, he was just flabbergasted.

He had to try it just one more time but he realized he was out of quarters. He walked down to the newsstand, which was quite a ways away and there was a long line that kept him waiting for his change. He finally got it, hustled back to the machine, and fed the fortune teller one last quarter. The readout said," Your name is John Smith and you just missed the 220 flight to Boston!"

Don't be distracted by unimportant things no matter how tempting they might be. Stay focused on your bread and butter, and teach what you know.

Chapter 33
Even Listen to a Fool

"When you talk, you are only repeating what you already know, but if you listen, you may learn something new."

—J.P. McEvoy

My grandfather used to say, "Even listen to a fool, for he may have listened to a wise man." My grandfather was no fool but we both liked that saying, and for that reason I don't discourage anyone from contributing (within reason) when I'm teaching.

Just because someone has less experience than you do doesn't mean that they can't teach you something. In folklore throughout the world, the fool often represents a blissful emptiness—a state of being without assumption, pretense, or ego. And because the fool comes to every situation with untrained eyes, he or she makes unexpectedly wise observations. You might assume that beginners don't have much to add or teach, but if you take this attitude then you will miss out on many moments of epiphany. There have been countless times when a student made an observation in class about a different way to employ a technique, for instance, that I had never even thought of. Of course, I always knowingly said, "Well, of course," even though it may have been a revelation to me.

Listening to everyone doesn't mean heeding everyone, but hear people out and you'll learn a lot. Your martial arts skills are one thing, but people skills are far more important. You will do well to remember that ancient martial arts saying, "Every[one] is my teacher."

Chapter 34
Be Thankful for Everyone

You may get along famously with some of the people you meet because there is an instant connection between you. Other people, not so much. But you know, that's okay. You can learn from everybody because everybody has natural talents. The more aware you are of other peoples' strengths and weaknesses, the more you will learn about the human condition. And you can benefit from others' life experiences and try to make the best out of each and every relationship you have, both on and off the floor. Being thankful for everyone who crosses your path will make you a better teacher and a more compassionate human being.

Chapter 35
Be Somebody

Be somebody who makes everybody feel like somebody. Every class should be a private lesson, or at least that's how your students should feel. How do we make every lesson a private lesson? Maintain great eye contact by scanning the room as you teach and make an effort to connect with each student at some point during the class. Be aware of your body language and your position in the class as you move around the room. Learn all of your students' names and be sure to praise them by name in front of the class throughout the lesson as well as individually when you walk by. Saying "Great job, Dave," or "Well done, Jean," can go a long way toward making a student feel important and appreciated. And do your best to nurture that sacred space between you and your student. That space is what makes your relationship unique and shows them that you care. While you're teaching your class, don't look up and see the group; look up and see the individual.

Chapter 36
Stay Positive

Yes, we have a challenging job, but stay positive and think the best of everyone. Beautiful things will happen in your life when you distance yourself from negativity. The experiences that you are waiting for and hoping for, like a breakthrough for a student, tend to arrive at the most unexpected moments. Keep your eyes open for these surprises. Progress, no matter how slow, should always be acknowledged and appreciated, and people respond far better to praise than they do to criticism.

Martial arts practice takes time. Take baby steps, just like Bill Murray's character in the film *What About Bob?* Take baby steps toward each technique, baby steps toward awareness, and baby steps toward focus. All of these baby steps, over a period of time, help your students recognize that they are making tremendous progress.

I tell our teachers and staff members to remember the letters *I* and *P*, which stand for *infinite patience* and *infinite positivity*. Have infinite patience with fellow teachers, with coworkers, parents, siblings, vendors, and of course students. When you practice infinite patience and infinite positivity, and you expect good things, then good things are bound to come. And there is hope even in the most challenging cases. Remember, in the words of Tertullian, the prolific early Christian author, "Hope is patience with the lamp lit."

Chapter 37
A Key to Retention is Culture

The secret to keeping students is to create a culture of support, positive energy, camaraderie, growth, learning, fun, and, most importantly, family. It's not about the next form. It's not about the next arm-bar. It's not about the next take down. It's about how your students feel at your school. If they feel happy, nurtured, and supported, then they will keep coming back. This kind of culture is not easily found outside the martial arts school, so you're offering a unique community to which your students can belong. Your students, regardless of age, should be excited the moment they pull into your parking lot. When they want to be a part of the culture you've created then you'll find that you have students for life.

Chapter 38
A Key to Retention is Cultivating Life Skills

The world can be a dark place, full of people looking to drag you down with them. If you can make your school a place where students can learn life skills as well as martial arts skills in a bright and encouraging environment, then your students will have even more impetus to study with you throughout the years.

For instance, you might notice that after weeks of practice a student confidently performs a technique, like a kata or a particular submission hold, in front of the entire class. Use that opportunity to both praise her and explain that she can channel that same confidence to make a sales call at work or present a report to her classmates. After all, a truly confident person is confident wherever she goes and in any environment.

The outside world can drain a person's batteries. Make your school a place where these batteries are recharged so that your students can go back into the world with renewed vigor. After your students finish class, they should be better equipped to handle life's challenges the next day, physically, mentally, and emotionally. Remind your students of the ways in which everything they learn on the dojo floor can be directly applied to their lives, and soon your dojo will become instrumental to their successes.

Chapter 39
Wants v. Needs

The difference between what a student wants and what a student needs can be vast, and often what a student wants is not what she needs at any given time, but great teachers masterfully balance the wants and needs of their students. Students, in order to learn and change, need to be continuously challenged, but they may not always want a challenge.

If you give a student too much of what he wants and too much of what he is good at then there may be little or no change or growth. Likewise, if you give a student too much of what he needs and he's not ready for it, you run the risk of losing that student. For instance, a new student may come in and all he wants to do is spar, but you know that he must learn certain techniques before he can spar safely and with control. You perhaps satisfy his wants and needs by having him spar slowly or by only using limited techniques that he's already familiar with.

Another example might be the student who always wants to learn something new or move on to the next thing rather than spending time on the much-needed fundamentals that she has yet to master. You perhaps deal with this situation by showing her a glimpse of how the advanced technique is just an extension of the fundamentals you are encouraging her to stick with. Remind her that if she commits to the fundamentals, she will eventually master the advanced techniques too.

Great teachers balance what the student wants and what the student needs and realize they're not always the same things.

Chapter 40
Never Speak Ill

If you are frustrated with your students, remember that they have put themselves in your world before you criticize them. They're trying. They're trying to improve and trying to learn, otherwise, they wouldn't be there. Respect that effort by never speaking ill of a student, not even in jest, not even to fellow teachers or staff members, and especially not to another student.

If some of your students exhibit behaviors that you want to change and that you know they want to change, then help them to change as kindly as you can. Mastery and effective teaching are about communicating compassionately with your students. Saint Francis de Sales once said, "Nothing is so strong as gentleness, nothing so gentle as real strength." Don't try to break your students down to build them back up; instead, elevate your students from where they are right now. I particularly like this advice from, J.M. Barrie, the author of *Peter Pan,* who writes, "Always be a little more kind than necessary"

Chapter 41
Transcend the Physical

Yes, in some ways, the martial arts are predicated on the physical: strength, technique, agility, and grace. However, if you really want students who remain loyal to your school and encourage their families and friends to study with you for generations to come too, then you must transcend the physical and teach your students the essence of the martial arts: practices to balance the mind, body, and spirit in perfect harmony.

After all, what is a student more likely to use on a daily basis? Front-kicks, punches, and choke holds? Or courtesy, respect, and patience? Don't develop the physical at the expense the mental and spiritual. Remember, our martial training is not one-dimensional, it's multi-dimensional. If you can teach your students how to cultivate mental, emotional, and spiritual strengths through your physical curriculum, then they will understand that the martial arts are a way of being. They'll use their martial arts skills to navigate their lives, and they may make you their life-long guide and encourage their loved ones to do the same.

Chapter 42
Surprised is OK, but Don't Take it Personally

Never let your emotion go beyond surprise when someone wrongs you or doesn't do what you expect. And consider this as food for thought: what if you let go of all your expectations? In *The Four Agreements*, Don Miguel Ruiz writes that we shouldn't take anything personally. We all like to take the good things that people say about us personally, but when someone says something negative about us, we tend not to want to own it. We might even disparage the person who hurt us, even if it wasn't intentional. Practice taking nothing personally, neither the good nor the bad, because someone who loves you today could feel entirely different tomorrow. When people fail to meet your expectations, you suffer. Practice not taking anything personally and letting go of these expectations.

You have no control over other people's behavior, but you can control your own and decide how to react. No matter how stressful a situation is, experiencing the moment without taking it personally will give you a better handle on it, and this will make you the kind of person that your students want to emulate. Keep on an even keel, sail through the surprise, and release the rest to the wind. If your students witness your positive attitude during challenging times then they are more likely to stay with you through the journey.

Chapter 43
Be a Benevolent Dictator

I am a firm believer in running your school as a benevolent dictator, not as a democracy. I don't believe in parent focus groups telling the sensei how to run things because the sensei is the person with the expertise. That doesn't mean that you ignore and scorn all feedback. You listen when people need to talk, but realize that you are the one who knows how the martial arts work. You are the one who knows how to teach your students. What you say goes! But a benevolent dictatorship need not detract from your school's culture of support or excellent student service.

You don't have to be best buds with your students. You should be friendly, not familiar. The vast majority of your students should see you for what you are: their martial arts instructor. Be judicious with how you present yourself and how much you share with your students, especially new students. For example, don't talk about your personal life with your students. Don't use the class as a captive audience for your venting or performance. Be available for support, but don't fall into the role of therapist. You do not want to compromise the sacred space of the teacher-student relationship. If you do, then you may find yourself giving your students what they want rather than what they need. They may feel comfortable challenging your authority, which becomes a real problem when students believe they're ready to advance but you don't.

With all the access to social media, it will behoove you to be exceptionally careful with what you chose to share. Trust me, it does nothing for the student - teacher relationship if the student knows what you had for dinner last night or what time you took a nap! If you like to use social media for both personal and business purposes, then a great way to work around this is to have a personal account set to private and a public, professional account just for business. And even if your personal account is just friends, still use your head and post responsibly.

Chapter 44

See Yourself in Every Student You Teach

It is so easy to become frustrated when a student doesn't meet your expectations. But think about it—how were you as a white belt? As a green belt? A brown belt? I know I was pretty bad. Honestly, I can remember what I was like and it wasn't pretty.

See yourself, as you were as a beginner, in every student you teach. Remember what it was like to come to all of this new and you'll have more patience and a better understanding of what each and every student is going through. We can be guilty of attributing black-belt-thinking to white belts students. White belts are white belts so of course they think like white belts and they act like white belts. That should not be a surprise. Remember that they have a beginner's mind, and really, that's a sacred thing. Zen Buddhists believe that we should go through life with *Shoshin*, or *beginner's mind*, so we can be open to learning and the nuance of experience in every moment, unburdened by preconceptions, expectation, or prejudice. Embrace beginner's mind, theirs and yours.

Chapter 45
Three Key Questions

On occasion, a parent or guardian may say that their child does not want to come to class and that it is difficult to get them to your school. This can really be a challenge even for the most supportive parents. We know that children are present-focused. If you offer a child a dollar now or ten dollars tomorrow, they are most likely to take the dollar now. That is why, at our school, we literally enroll the parents but we teach the kids.

Here are three key questions to ask a parent or guardian if you are dealing with this type of situation. Do you believe in the curriculum we are teaching your child? Are you comfortable with the atmosphere we provide for your child's education? And lastly, are you comfortable with the role models we provide for your child?

It is your job to make sure that the answer to all three questions is always *yes*. When a parent does answer *yes* to all three of these questions, they are much more likely to dig in and get their child back on track. As a teacher and school owner, make sure that there are truly no finer role models, curriculum, or atmosphere in your community. Make your school the optimum environment for parents and guardians to bring their children to learn, grow, and develop.

Chapter 46
Those Who Dare

"Those who dare to teach or lead must never cease to learn."

—John Cotton Dana

I love this quote from Dana because, as martial artists, aren't we students for life? True masters are students first and teachers second. Your continuous learning will make you a better person and teacher. If you don't have a teacher, then find one. You have a responsibility to do so both to your students and to yourself.

Years ago, I had the honor of touring the People's Republic of China as a guest of the Chinese government with my teacher, George Mattson and our headmaster Kanei Uechi, along with an entourage of other Okinawan masters. We were there to trace the roots of our style of karate. I noticed that when our hosts spoke of one of the great masters of the past, they would describe him as "man of the pen, man of the sword." They explained that this was the highest compliment they could pay a true martial artist. Martial artists were warriors but true masters were also educated, literate, intelligent, and continued to learn their entire lives. They were the pen and sword in accord.

Be the best student and teacher you can possibly be by always learning like the great masters. The Internet and social media make it easier than ever to gather information and further your knowledge and you can learn a lot from the world outside the martial arts as well. Everyone you meet is your teacher and you can make unexpected connections at any moment.

Section 5

Student Service Tips

Chapter 47
Student Service Tips

Yes, we teach martial arts, but please remember that we teach people first and martial arts second. Techniques and transactions are far less important than relationships, and great student service is built upon great relationships. The better you treat your students, the better they will respond to your instruction. It's really that simple. In this section, we'll cover tips for maintaining that sacred space between you and your students while making them feel cared for, special, and unique.

Chapter 48
Litmus Test

As a kind of litmus test, look in the mirror before going home for the day, and with no one else around, ask yourself this question: *Did I do the very best I could for each and every student that walked through my door today?* If the answer is *yes*, then you can go home and sleep well. If the answer feels like a *no*, then explore the reasons why. Be honest with yourself. *What more could I have done? Could I have made better connections? Could I have spent more time with each and every student? Could I have been more encouraging?* Use this as a time for reflection. Set yourself some clear, achievable, and practical goals to improve as a teacher. For instance, work on eye contact or make a point of praising your class at least three times each session. Come up with a game plan before you leave so you can go home, recharge, and wake up knowing your mission the next day.

If you take the time to look in the mirror and ask yourself these questions, you will be more self-aware as a teacher and at the end of the day, you'll be able to move forward with an easy mind and watch your school grow.

Chapter 49

First Impression

We all have different ways of welcoming a new student into our schools, and I am a huge believer in the personal touch, regardless of whether or not you've already been corresponding via email with the prospective student or their guardian.

In Hank Trisler's wonderful book, *No Bull Selling*, he shares a template that he uses for the personal notes that he writes and sends to each and every one of his new customers. The handwritten note is a nice touch because it's more than just a gesture of courtesy—it's an act of kindness that shows that you care and helps to eliminate any buyer's remorse on the client's part. I cannibalized Trisler's template to draw-up my own personal note, which I hand write to every new student upon enrollment.

Dear, Mr. and Mrs. Lee,
This is a personal note to thank you for your
courtesy and the trust and confidence you placed in

me by enrolling Bruce in our school. I am proud to have him as a student!

I know that Bruce will benefit and that you will be pleased with the results of his training.

If you should ever need or want special assistance of any kind, please do not hesitate to ask me. My door will always be open to you. Welcome to our school.

Sincerely,

Buzz Durkin

This note, aside from being handwritten, is customized, personalized, and addressed and mailed by hand. The note shows that you truly appreciate your new students, sets a positive tone for the relationship, and lets them know *I'm here for you, whatever you may need.* Get in the habit of sending out these handwritten notes to every one of your new students, and mean it. This small effort will make a big impression and yield huge dividends.

Chapter 50
Cards

Always keep stamped postcards and note cards in a convenient place right near your desk. This way, it'll make it easy to send notes and cards before you leave for the night. The easier you make it, the more likely you are to do it. Student service is always best when it's unexpected. Of course your students expect you to be thinking of them while they're in class and right in front of you, but it's when they are away from the school and they hear from you that it's most impactful. It shows that you are thinking of them even on your own time.

At my dojo, we have thank you cards, you've-been-awesome cards, birthday cards, missed-you-in-class cards, congratulations cards, and on and on, for all occasions, all hand-written and hand-stamped. People love getting these cards in the mail because, let's face it, most of what comes in the mail is either junk or bills. A personal note from the martial arts teacher is refreshing and warmly received. If we are sending a note to a junior student, we always address it to the student in care of her parents unless it is a postcard which can be read without opening. Both kids and adults enjoy getting this type of communication. Don't we all?

Your cards don't necessarily have to be restricted to milestones or in-class performance. One week in class, we were talking about posture: head up, look up, and the like. Then, a week or so later, an adult student asked if he could see me after class and tell me a story. I said, "Of course." Well, we just had a big snowstorm and he was walking across the street when his bag slipped down over his shoulder. He looked down and something told him just at that moment "Head up, look up." He looked up in-time to step out of the way of a car just about to hit him. He told me he was so thankful that we talked about those subjects in class because if he hadn't looked up at that exact moment, then he surely would've been hit.

I listened and thanked him for sharing that story with me. That night before I left the dojo, I dropped this simple little note in the mail: "Glad you kept your head up."

Another day, two adult students came to class so excited because they had both just purchased new cars and they were delighted with their new rides. The next day, I purchased a $50 gas card and a book of car washes and wrote two notes saying just three words: "Congratulations! Happy motoring." I put the gas card in with one note and the book of car washes in the other and happily mailed them off.

Think of kind and creative ways to reach out to your students and let them know that you're thinking about them, even outside of class.

Chapter 51
No "No Problem"

Get out of the habit of saying, "No problem." It's always better to say "My pleasure." When you think about it, saying *no problem* in place of a pleasantry like *you're welcome* is a silly way to talk because if you're serving your students then it should be your pleasure.

In the town where I live, we have a beautiful country club. One day, I went in and the lady behind the desk smiled and asked me, "How can I help you?"

"I would like to purchase two gift certificates, please," I told her.

She said, "No problem. Would you like to pay by cash or credit card?"

"Credit card."

"No problem," she said. "Would you like two envelopes or one?"

"Two please."

"No problem. Should I write the names of the recipients on the cards?"

"No thank you—I'll do that."

"No problem."

You know, by the time I was through with the purchase, I was beginning to have a problem. That's when it struck me, why even bring up problems during an exchange of goods and services? Think and speak positively.

Martial artists are people of service and we should serve with joy. It was Mahatma Gandhi who said, "Service which is rendered without joy helps neither the servant nor the served." And it was Albert Schwetzer who said "The purpose of human life is to serve and show compassion and the will to help others." Make service a pleasure, not a problem.

Chapter 52
Answering the Phone

You've probably heard this before but it's so critical that it bears repeating: smile when you pick up the phone. But do more than that—be positive throughout the entire conversation. At my school, instead of answering the phone by asking, "How may I help you?" we simply say, "I can help you." My idea is that if I can't get you the answer then I will lead you to someone who can.

Too many people who answer the phone use *demand language* instead of *request language,* for instance, saying, "Hold on," when what they should say is, "May I ask you to hold for a moment?" If you need something from the other party, it is much more polite to respectfully ask them to do what you need rather than making demands on them which could sound rude, especially if you aren't careful with your tone.

We always try to pick up the phone by the third ring and if someone requests information and ends their conversation by saying, "Thank you," then we never just reply, "You're welcome." Instead we say, "Thank you!" as well. It's important that we are always the last to say *thank you*, because it's the small courtesies that sweeten life and make for a more pleasant school.

Chapter 53
Gratitude and Appreciation

Never expect gratitude but always show appreciation. Do good things because it's good to do good things, not because you're expecting any kind of thanks. You are not the center of your students' universe—they are. They put themselves first. Don't worry about it. If they don't show gratitude then what difference does it make to you really? But if you do get a little "thank you," then consider it a bonus.

You, on the other hand, should always show appreciation even for the smallest things, even for your students just showing up to class. My school is in New Hampshire, so on cold winter nights it would be easy for them to stay home, sit by the fireplace, and drink hot chocolate. But no, my students choose not to do that; they make the conscious effort to brave the cold and come to class, and man, do I appreciate that! I show my appreciation by giving them my best and by telling them how much I appreciate their presence. Not a class goes by that I don't thank each and every student for coming to the dojo, working hard, and being cooperative. Show appreciation for even the smallest kindness and watch how your students respond. You're going to love it.

Chapter 54
A Great Philosophy

One business person I admire is Harvey Mackay, New York Times best-selling author of *Swim with the Sharks without Being Eaten Alive*. On several occasions when I've gone to see him speak, Mackay suggested that we should "[t]hink long-term and think in human terms in every interaction." If I make a decision today, then what are the effects of that decision going to be five days from now? Five weeks from now? Five months from now? Five years from now? A decision that you make today may give you immediate satisfaction and or gratification, but how is it going to play out in the future? Because of a decision you make today, will a student speak poorly about you in five years? Or will he send his cousin and all his other relatives to see you and to learn from you? Think about it.

Secondly, think in human terms. Yes, we run a business, but each and every one of us teaches people first, martial arts second. Everyone we deal with has a heart, soul, and emotions. Be sensitive to that. If you treat everyone with care and compassion while being of service, then people will remember that and always speak highly of you.

Think long-term and think in human terms. Don't be impetuous in your actions. Take your time and consider how your behavior affects you and the people in your life.

Chapter 55
Happy Staff = Happy Students

It's true that people come first and your students are your primary focus, but your staff is just as important. Take care of your staff's wants, needs, and desires first and they will take better care of your students. The happier your staff is, the more their happiness is reflected in your students. The pack follows the lead dog, so that means if you're in a good mood, then your staff will be in a good mood, and in turn your students will be in a good mood too. You must educate, motivate, and compensate your staff, and go above the call of duty. Personalize their perks, spend time with them, and make sure they know you care for them. Happy staff equals happy students.

Chapter 56
Names, Please

"What's in a name? That's what we ask ourselves in childhood when we write the name we are told is ours."

—*James Joyce*

Names are powerful—they are our identity, so you should always address your students by name. There are eight billion people in the world and each one is unique and each person wants to feel special. The first step toward making your students feel important is to make the effort to remember their names. Each time you greet a student by name, it strengthens your personal connection with that student. If I notice someone in the dojo who I don't know, then I'll make darn sure I find out who they are before I go and greet them. If the person is there to observe a student, then I make a connection with them regarding the student they came to observe—everyone at your dojo should feel personally welcomed. You want everyone to feel like they belong.

I've been going to the same gym for twelve years, and even though I check-in every morning, no one ever greets me by my name. The strangest part about this is that when I check-in, my name and my picture both come up on the screen right in front of the person behind the counter, and most of the time that person won't even look up. My friends at this gym quite often notice the same thing and lament the fact that a personal greeting would go a long way toward making them feel like they're more a part of the club. This is why my teachers and staff make a point of getting up, reaching out, and greeting everyone who comes through the door every day, every class, by name. The hard, cold business fact of the matter is that the happier someone is at your business establishment, the more money they will happily spend there. It astounds me that so many businesses don't understand this simple concept.

The computer you're sitting in front of will be there at 10 o'clock at night, but that guest who walks through your door or that student who comes in will be long gone. But the computer will still be there. Not a class goes by without me greeting everyone who comes through our doors, regardless of what I'm doing. I look at it this way—a person coming into my school is just like someone coming into my home. Would I ever refuse to acknowledge anyone who came into my home? Wouldn't I say, "Hello," and welcome them inside? So think of your school as your home and be hospitable—greet your guests and students personally, address them by name, and make everyone feel like they belong.

Chapter 57
Stand Up

If you have a program director or a receptionist at a workstation, or in an office, always make sure that they stand when someone comes to see them. The same goes for the boss. Standing when someone speaks to you or comes into your office shows respect. It shows they have your undivided attention. It's a small gesture, but it's noticeable and it's important. Again, the great poet Emily Dickinson is right when she says, "If you take care of the small things, the big things will take care of themselves." Standing up when you speak with someone is a small thing, but it soon gives way to a much bigger thing—a reputation for outstanding student service.

Years ago, I was traveling to Okinawa and I was fortunate enough to be flying first class with Japan Airlines. My traveling companion and I were supposed to meet in the first class lounge. I arrived early and the agent behind the desk stood up and politely greeted me as I walked through the door. I waited inside for a few minutes but then went back outside into the main corridor, looking for my friend. My traveling companion was late, so again I walked back into the lounge and the person behind the desk stood up, smiled, and greeted me by name this time. I went back and forth through that door about a half dozen times and every time that agent stood up. It would've been so easy for him to just sit down with an, *oh, you again*, attitude, but he didn't. He paid me attention, respect, and courtesy, all by this simple gesture. It impressed me so much that I made it part of my business ethos.

Chapter 58
No

With regards to customer service, the word *no* is probably the ugliest word in the English language. It's so abrupt, so cutting, so demoralizing. Whenever you can, avoid the word *no*. Find a more pleasant way of giving someone negative information. For example, a student might ask, "Is there a 5 o'clock class that I can take today?" If the answer is no, then you could say something like, "There is not a 5 o'clock class today for your rank, but we do have a 6:30 or 7:45 class that you can attend." The positive spin makes you seem that much more accommodating.

Chapter 59
Creativity

James Murdoch says, "Believe in better." Dr. Frank I. Luntz also uses this mantra in his book *Win*, and it should be yours too. "Believe in better" is a motto at our school because I believe that even if your service is excellent there is always room for improvement. This in turn has given way to another motto: "If it ain't broke, break it," because it's not enough to just believe in better—you have to break the mold and be creative.

For years, when a student was sick, had a baby, or celebrated a special event, we would always send them flowers. This gesture was always appreciated but after a week or so the flowers would of course die. Then I thought, *How can I make that experience even better?* When I took that moment to consider how I could improve our school's service, it dawned on me—I brought a gross of our Buzz Durkin's Karate School coffee mugs to our local florist with the instructions that whenever they sent out an arrangement to one of our students, it would be in one of our mugs. Now, the flowers would still last maybe a week, but my students will have the mugs for years and think of my school every morning when they drink their coffee. When you believe in better, you come up with creative ways to show your devotion to your students even when there are no problems to speak of, and that's what makes stand-out service.

Chapter 60
5:00 PM

It's 5:00 PM and you've been at your school since 10:00 AM. Sometime, preferably in the late afternoon, find time to get in your car, drive around the block, park, and then walk back into your school one more time. You'll be amazed by the sights, sounds, and scents that attack your senses: jackets strewn all over the changing room floor, a faucet or shower still trickling, shoes scattered pell-mell in the shoe room, which may not smell like a bed of roses.

As a teacher with your extensive martial arts training, you have learned to maintain a beginner's mind. Use it. By doing this exercise, you'll see your school as a beginner would, walking in for the first time. It's only natural that, after being in the dojo for hours, you might miss the little messes that accumulate throughout the day unless you make an effort to see your school anew. That's why, regardless of how clean and fresh your locker room, changing room, and bathroom usually are, make a point of keeping them pristine. Check them first thing in the morning and then make someone responsible for checking them on the hour throughout the day and keeping them that way. It's amazing what a five-year-old can do to a room in less than five minutes, not to mention what a forty-five-year-old can do with a can of foot powder.

Chapter 61
Letting Go

Students are going to leave you. I haven't met a teacher yet who has forever kept every student who began with her. And you know what, that's okay. It's not important—that's life! What is important, however, is how we talk about these former students, how we think about them, and how we act around them.

Here is the secret: don't complain or call them quitters. Be thankful that they started with you in the first place. They have enriched your life because they taught you something about human nature. They helped pay the bills and supported your school so you could continue to teach.

I send a personal note to everyone who stops training with me. I'm not talking about an exit survey; I'm talking about a personal, hand-written note just like the notes I send to new and continuing students, and I suggest you do the same. Tell them you enjoyed having them at your school and let them know the door will always be open for their return. Mean it! When you do this, your former students will appreciate it and they are more likely to think highly of your school. They may come back when the time is better for them in their lives. They may send their neighbors or relatives to train with you.

Keep the entirety of the student-teacher relationship positive, even the end. You should be able to go anywhere where you may run into former students, holding your head up high, able to look anyone in the eye. Conduct yourself in such a way that you know that you treated all your students with dignity and respect, and told them that you value them as unique, wonderful people who you are proud to have met and trained at your school.

Chapter 62
Err on the Side of Formality

I have found that it is always better to err on the side of formality when dealing with people. Refer to the people who visit your school as *Mr. So-and-So*, or *Mrs. So-and-So*, and remember that some women prefer the more progressive and politically correct "*Ms.*" (pronounced *Miz*), which side-steps the whole appellation-based-on-marital-status issue that men don't have to deal with. It's ok, even respectful, to ask if they have a preference. Most of the parents who come to my school are much younger than I am but I still refer to them as Mr., Mrs., Miss, or Ms. because it shows respect and courtesy. Don't address them by their first names unless they implore you to do so. Anyone who knows me knows that I am not a very formal person but I still adhere to this policy and require my staff to do the same.

Once I had a young, twenty-something salesman who was just starting out stop by my school to sell me something. He knew my last name since our building is called "The Durkin Building," yet when he came into my office he kept addressing me as "Buzz." I didn't think he knew me well enough to call me by my first name; it showed a lack of respect and felt a little too familiar. I know he meant no disrespect, but it just didn't sit right with me, and consequently I didn't purchase what he was selling.

Interestingly enough, he came back several times to see me and he had a good product which I eventually purchased. After getting to know him a little better, he asked me why I didn't buy from him on his first visit. I told him as nicely as possible that he was too informal and he didn't know me well enough to call me by my first name, and being the smart young man he was, he got it. We now enjoy a wonderful relationship and he has become quite successful. To this day he considers me a business mentor.

Chapter 63
Never Give Up on a Student

Our school's foundational philosophy is that we never give up on a student, and this philosophy will serve any school owner well. If you believe in your heart of hearts that training at your school is a great thing, then why would you ever stop fighting for a student?

Never give up on a student whether they are actively training or not. Encourage students, current and former, to come back through personal notes, newsletters, training-tips, and on and on. If they are currently training with you, then go that extra step through private lessons or extra-help before or after a class. If they have stopped training, continue your support as though they will be back. If you really think training at your school will make your students and former students into better people, then don't you have an obligation to get them back on track? I think so. Your commitment and perseverance will help both your students and your school flourish.

Chapter 64
Durkin's Do's and Don'ts

Don't	**Do**
Don't...think of work as a transaction.	*Do*...build relationships.
Don't...assume anything.	*Do*…consistently communicate.
Don't…be short tempered and abrupt.	*Do*…develop infinite positivity and patience.
Don't…hide from or avoid people.	*Do*…be accessible.
Don't…expect gratitude.	*Do*… show appreciation, always.

Don't…say, "No problem."

Do… say, "My pleasure."

Don't…think any job in your school is beneath you.

Do…what needs to be done and set an example.

Don't…run your school like a democracy.

Do…run your school like a benevolent dictator.

Don't…focus on money.

Do…focus on your students and service.

Don't…ignore anyone.

Do…go out of your way to greet everyone by name.

Don't…be bound by tradition.

Do…respect tradition.

Don't…be timid about anything to do with your school, including tuition.

Do…be confident in all matters, including your value and your tuition.

Section 6

Best Business Practices

Chapter 65
Simple, but Not Easy

"Life is really simple, but we insist on making it complicated."

—*Confucius*

This section deals with five best business practices essential for the school owner's success and happiness in the long term. They are simple but not necessarily easy. They require self-discipline, and if you commit to the practice of these habits, you will be rewarded and fulfilled as a teacher, a martial artist, and as a contented and respected person.

Chapter 66
Focus on Service

I remember my first meeting with Nicholas Cokinos. He was so sure of himself when he told me, "Buzz, don't focus on money; focus on taking care of your students, first and foremost. And if you do a good job with that, the money will follow. It will come in the doors, the windows, and the heating vents." I've learned through the years that he was oh-so-correct!

I have known many individuals through the years who opened schools with money as their prime motivator. Ultimately, all of their schools failed because their main focus was just that, money, not service, and it's a service-driven business.

One saying from an unknown source that always has been meaningful to me is, "He is a true master of men who behaves as if he is their servant." Serve others because it is the right thing to do and happiness and success will follow.

Chapter 67
Build Reserves

In *A Passion for Success,* Kazuo Inamori advises that you build reserves but operate as if you have no reserves. I've followed this advice and learned that it really is a great philosophy.

We martial arts school owners are a funny breed. We talk about self-discipline and self-control, but we do not always exercise these practices in our personal lives. Often times, when school owners receive a 'paid in full' for a twelve month or twenty-four month program, they spend that windfall of money right away and are then indebted for a large number of lessons owed. It's easy to forget that money paid in advance is unearned income.

The best thing to do when this type of up-front income comes in is to put it in reserve and disperse it to yourself as the lessons are taught. This will help you build reserves which you may need some day, and if nothing else, these reserves afford you more financial freedom. Many school owners think that just because they had a windfall they can buy this or they can spend money on that and then they spend wildly. Be smart and save appropriately.

Chapter 68
Save a Small Percentage

Over twenty-five years ago, I met a fellow martial artist from Korea and we became friends. When we met, he was alone in a new country, his wife and two children still in Korea, and he was learning English. His dream was to become a successful martial arts school owner in The U.S.– the land of opportunity. From the start of his career, he did something that really impressed me. He put 5% of his total monthly income into a savings account, and then he continued this year after year. When his school became more successful, he put aside 10% of his gross monthly income. He pretended as if he never even earned it and had it automatically taken out. He never wanted to see it. Now he's a multimillionaire, and imagine, when he started his business he was still just learning the language and lifestyle of his new country, but because of his dedication, savvy, and self-discipline he overcame these challenges with enormous success.

If you have the self-discipline to save like my friend, it can be a great thing. And the best way to do it, of course, is never to see this money. Try to set it up, either through your third-party billing or direct deposit, so that a certain percentage is diverted into a separate savings account automatically. Saving a little can add up to a lot.

Chapter 69
Bricks and Mortar

I was fortunate enough to build my school and design it to my exact specifications, but I rented a space for the fourteen years prior and every single bit of that rent went out the door, right into the landlord's bank account.

However, if you own your establishment then every payment you make brings you one step closer to owning a valuable asset. Don't be overwhelmed by the thought of buying a building. Often times the monthly mortgage payment can be less than or equal to what you may be paying for rent. Buy something, build something, own something. You will have a martial arts school as well as a building, and these two separate entities can provide many opportunities. Maybe you will end up with some space to lease within your building which will help you pay off the mortgage. Owning the building offers many tax advantages as well. Someday, way down the road if you are thinking of retirement, you may choose to sell your school and continue ownership of your building. You may choose to sell the building and keep the school. Either way, you will have options.

Chapter 70
Joyful, Grateful, and Humble

Always strive to be joyful, grateful, and humble in your dealings with everyone, both in business and in life. I learned the value of practicing these virtues from my late mentor, Nicholas Cokinos, and all the great masters. Confucius writes, "Choose a job you love and you will never have to work a day in your life." And when you think about it, who has a better job than we do? We get to have a positive influence on people's lives every day by teaching them how to harmonize mind, body, and spirit. How did we get it so good? We're even our own bosses. And aren't all true masters happy? I think back upon my late Grandmaster Kanei Uechi, and he always smiled in the face of challenges, no matter how serious. I've learned that the happiest people don't have the best of everything, they just make the best of everything. Be joyful in the present moment.

On gratitude, Zig Zigler writes, "Of all the attitudes we can acquire, surely the attitude of gratitude is the most important and by far the most life changing." Look at everything you have—I'll bet that you have a lot more than you realized. Be grateful for all of it, including your personal relationships, your business relationships, and the support of your wonderful students who believe in you. Take some advice from the great writer Alice Walker and always express your gratitude: "'Thank you' is the best prayer that anyone could say. I say that one a lot. Thank you expresses extreme gratitude, humility, and understanding." Be thankful for the unlimited potential that being a martial arts teacher gifts you.

And humility is our last business practice—control your ego, control yourself. Don't brag, don't show off, and as your school grows, don't let your ego grow with it. Let others talk about your skills, and let your reputation precede you. Theodore Roosevelt once said, "People don't care how much you know until they know how much you care," so serve people humbly and that will draw people to you.

Conclusion

ENDING WORDS

I began this book with a quote by Ralph Waldo Emerson, "What lies behind us and what lies before us are tiny matters compared to what lies within us," and I am ending this book with a quote by Miyamoto Musashi, "Seek nothing outside of yourself." Both of these quotes have meant so much to me in my life and in my career because they remind me that any one person has what it takes to be successful. You have what it takes, and what it takes is within you. And you are the only person who can truly stop yourself from being successful. Don't stop yourself; carry on and be great. Embody unyielding commitment and perseverance. Exude confidence and let yourself be truly passionate about your work. You will find that success is out there, just waiting.

All the best.

"There is nothing outside of yourself that can enable you to get better, stronger, richer, quicker, or smarter. Everything is within.
Everything exists.
Seek nothing outside of yourself."
—*Miyamoto Musashi*

ABOUT THE AUTHOR

Buzz Durkin is a ninth degree black belt in Okinawan Uechi-ryu Karate. For more than four decades he has been the headmaster of Buzz Durkin's Karate School, which is one of the most successful traditional martial arts schools in North America. His school has won school of the year and martial art facility of the year multiple times. Durkin is a charter member of the Uechi-ryu Hall of Fame and a member of the World Martial Arts Hall of Fame. Durkin is on the board of directors of the Educational Funding Company and the governing board of the World Martial Arts Federation. He has appeared on the cover of several international magazines including *Martial Arts Professional* and *Uechi Newsline*.

Durkin is internationally recognized as an expert in student service and as such has been the keynote speaker at numerous International Martial Arts conventions. He has been a guest speaker for the United States Martial Arts Association, The Educational Funding Company, The World Martial Arts Federation and the International Uechi Karate Federation to name a few. His ability to relate to people and his understanding of human nature are known and recognized worldwide making him a much sought after speaker and consultant not only in the martial arts field but in the academic and corporate fields as well. He is known in the martial arts field as the "Retention King" for his ability to ensure student longevity of study.

Durkin is a Vietnam combat veteran who received both his Bachelor of Science degree and his MBA from Boston College. He lives in Atkinson, NH with his wife of forty years, Judy.

For more information on Buzz Durkin and his school visit: www.BuzzDurkin.com.